D0048577

Somalia

Library Resource Center
Renton Technical College
3000 NE 4th St.
Renton, WA 98056-4195

Brookings Occasional Papers

Somalia

State Collapse, Multilateral Intervention, and Strategies for Political Reconstruction

Terrence Lyons and Ahmed I. Samatar

THE BROOKINGS INSTITUTION
Washington, D.C.

327
.730677
LYONS
1995

Brookings Occasional Papers

THE BROOKINGS INSTITUTION is a private nonprofit organization devoted to research, education, and publication on important issues of domestic and foreign policy. Its principal purpose is to bring knowledge to bear on the major policy problems facing the American people.

On occasion Brookings staff members produce research papers that warrant immediate circulation as contributions to the public debate on current issues of national importance. Because of the speed of their production, these Occasional Papers are not subjected to all of the formal review procedures established for the Institution's research publications, and they may be revised at a later date. As in all Brookings publications, the judgments, conclusions, and recommendations presented in the Papers are solely those of the authors and should not be attributed to the trustees, officers, or other staff members of the Institution.

Copyright © 1995 by
THE BROOKINGS INSTITUTION
1775 Massachusetts Avenue, N.W., Washington, D.C.

ISBN 0-8157-5351-9

Library of Congress Catalog Number 95-70292

9 8 7 6 5 4 3 2 1

Acknowledgments

The authors would like to thank Zebib Bekure, Katharina Vogeli, and Jennifer Nix for their research assistance and Macalester College Office of International Studies and Programming for its support.

Research for this study was funded in part by the Carnegie Corporation of New York. We are very grateful for its support.

Contents

Somalia

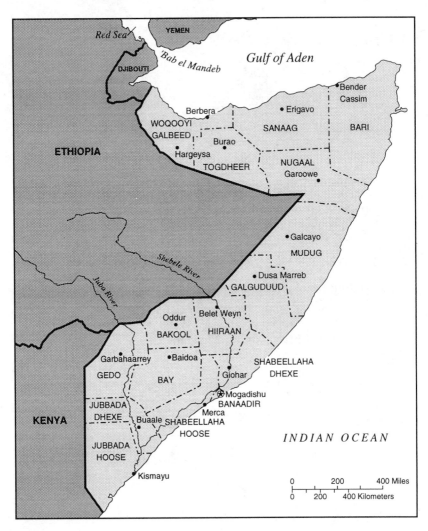

Source: Library of Congress, *Somalia: A Country Study* (Government Printing Office, 1992), p. xx.

Somalia: Ethnic Groups

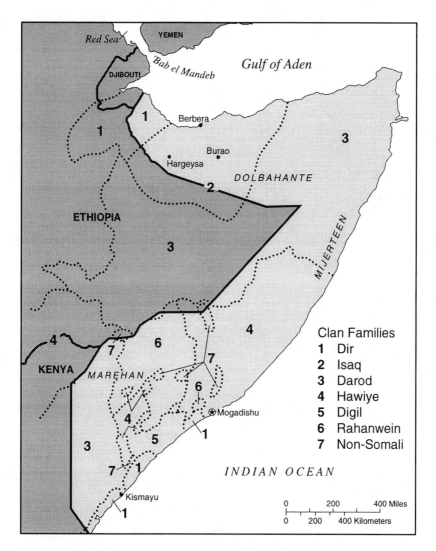

Clan Families
1 Dir
2 Isaq
3 Darod
4 Hawiye
5 Digil
6 Rahanwein
7 Non-Somali

Source: International Institute for Strategic Studies, *Strategic Survey, 1989–90* (London: IISS, 1990), p. 86. Reprinted by permission of Oxford University Press.

1

State Collapse and the International System

Artificial states without a strong social base of support, resources, or popular legitimacy often survived during the cold war thanks to superpower patronage and international norms that favored stability and sovereignty. Several of those states, however, collapsed in the 1990s, as external support was withdrawn and societal demands for economic advancement and better governance increased. State collapse occurs when structure, authority, legitimate power, law, and political order fall apart, leaving behind a civil society that lacks the ability to rebound to fill the vacuum. The structures of legitimate order therefore must be reconstituted in some form, old or new. Sometimes this requirement leads to anarchy, but other times legitimacy devolves to local groups. The demise of a state is inherently linked to a breakdown of social coherence on an extensive level as civil society can no longer create, aggregate, and articulate the supports and demands that are the foundations of the state. Without the state, society breaks down and without social structures, the state cannot survive.[1]

State collapse is not a short-term phenomenon but a cumulative, incremental process similar to a degenerative disease. Governments lose their ability to exercise legitimate authority unevenly over territory. Certain regions decompose or fall away from central control, as happened in northern Somalia in the late 1980s, while others remain within the government's realm. States may also collapse unevenly over time. Robert Kaplan quotes a resident of Freetown as saying that "the government in Sierra Leone has no writ after dark."[2] A state may lose its ability to exercise authority over some issues while maintaining influence over others. Some states disintegrate as cohesive economic entities while maintaining their political unity.[3]

The syndrome of state collapse often begins when a regime loses its ability to satisfy various demand-bearing groups in society as resources dry up. Dissatisfaction and opposition grow, resulting in the regime's increased use of security forces to maintain order. Sometimes the old government falls, and a successor regime, often based on the military, is capable of arresting the deterioration. In cases of state collapse, however, the degeneration is too widespread, and society is not able to rebound into a coherent foundation for the state. As a result the state collapses, and political and economic space retract, the center no longer has authority, and power withers away.[4]

In the 1990s, the nation-state, the most fundamental unit of international politics, has been under relentless pressure and questioning: the nation by new or revived cultural cleavages, the state by the forces of economic and political liberalization and heightened popular expectations.[5] Similarly, the tensions between the international norms of self-determination and territorial integrity have shifted in favor of self-determination.[6] National sovereignty and self-determination, however, are fraught with controversy because individuals and groups differ on their preferred sense of national identity.

Following the cold war, the historical tension between state sovereignty (relating authority to a defined territory) and "national sovereignty" (relating authority to a defined population) seems to be tilting to the disadvantage of the state.[7] As global concern for humanitarian issues increases, "The balance between sovereignty and suffering is shifting in favor of greater international sensitivity to the claims of those who suffer and greater impatience with the obstructionism of uncaring governments."[8] Secretary General Boutros Boutros-Ghali wrote in *An Agenda for Peace* that "the time of absolute and exclusive sovereignty . . . has passed; its theory was never matched by reality."[9]

With this new thinking about the limits to sovereignty has come a debate on the circumstances in which the international community may legitimately initiate "humanitarian intervention." Thomas Weiss and Larry Minear have suggested that "the world is poised between the Cold War and an embryonic new humanitarian order . . . in which life-threatening suffering and human rights abuses become legitimate international concerns irrespective of where they take place."[10] Stanley Hoffmann argued that "it is high time that the principle the UN has applied only to South Africa be generalized: No state should be able to claim that the way it treats its citizens is its sovereign right if this treatment is likely to create international tensions."[11]

Collapsed states pose a difficult challenge for the international community. The humanitarian consequences of political disintegration and anarchy in the form of famine, the destruction of economic infrastructure, human rights abuses, and refugees and internally displaced persons are clearly documented.[12] In an earlier time, massive human deprivation may have remained out of sight. The media age of the 1990s, with images broadcast instantly around the world, forces the world to encounter these tragedies, and an outraged populace often pressures its government to "do something."[13]

State breakdown also compels international action because the effects of the chaos cannot be limited to a small geographic region. Political disintegration generates instability and threatens neighboring states through refugee flows, the stimulation of illegal trade in weapons and other contraband, and because the communities imperiled by state collapse often cross borders and can appeal to neighboring groups for involvement. Because the international system of order is based on states, forces inimical to order move into the empty spaces where states no longer exist. Drug traffickers, money launderers, extremist political movements, and terrorist groups move into the vacuum in places like Afghanistan, Liberia, Burma, and Peru. Real international interests are at stake when states collapse, even without the public reaction to images of suffering that compel government officials in a democracy to respond. J. Brian Atwood, the administrator of the U.S. Agency for International Development, phrased the issue as the strategic threat of "chaos."

> Bosnia, Haiti, Rwanda. These troubling and unique crises in disparate regions of the globe share a common thread. They are the dark manifestations of a strategic threat that increasingly defines America's foreign policy challenge. Disintegrating societies and failed states with their civil conflicts and destabilizing refugee flows have emerged as the greatest menace to global stability.[14]

The Multilateral Response

International officials have responded to the challenge of state collapse by considering expanded multilateral peacekeeping or peace-enforcement operations. Peacekeeping is an innovation of the United Nations, improvised in response to the cold war constraints that prevented the more forceful actions originally envisioned by the drafters of the UN Charter. Peacekeeping falls somewhere in between Chapter VI (pacific settlement of disputes) and Chapter VII (enforcement) of the UN Charter, leading many to characterize such operations as "Chapter 6 1/2," or what Lester Pearson described as "an intermediate technique between merely passing resolutions and actually fighting."[15] Between 1945 and 1988 the United Nations conducted thirteen peacekeeping operations and gradually developed accepted principles.[16]

Paul F. Diehl enumerates the principal elements of traditional peace-keeping:

> Peacekeeping is . . . the imposition of neutral and lightly armed inter-position forces following a cessation of armed hostilities and with the permission of the state on whose territory these forces are deployed, in order to discourage a renewal of military conflict and promote an environment under which the underlying dispute can be resolved.[17]

Peacekeeping, because of the centrality of neutrality and the consent of the parties to its definition, is an action to reinforce a status quo, most often a cease-fire. Until the 1990s the United Nations largely eschewed involvement when conflict remained active or when peacekeepers were likely to see combat. During the cold war, the only UN operation that engaged in significant fighting and suffered significant casualties was that in the Congo (1960–64), and that operation nearly destroyed the organization.[18]

During the Persian Gulf War the international system expanded the contexts in which it would intervene dramatically. Faced with massive flows of Kurdish refugees in Turkey and Iran and large numbers of displaced Kurds in northern Iraq and vulnerable Shiites in southern Iraq, the Security Council declared in Resolution 688 of April 5, 1991, that a member government's repression of its people constituted a threat to international peace and security. Although refugee flows had the potential for destabilizing Turkey and Iran, the primary focus of Resolution 688 was the internal conflict.[19]

In the early 1990s, the traditional methods of UN peacekeeping evolved rapidly. The major powers, no longer limited by the cold war constraints that had incapacitated the United Nations for its first forty years, turned to the organization to respond to a host of new challenges, including the management of internal conflict and humanitarian emergencies.[20] As Brian Urquhart put it: "The new role of the Security Council, functioning for the first time as a collegial body as anticipated in the Charter rather than a battleground for the great powers, opens up a number of possibilities for regional conflict management."[21] The United Nations launched more peacekeeping operations between 1989 and 1994 than it had in its first forty-three years. In December 1994 more than 73,000 authorized military personnel were serving under UN command. The budget for peacekeeping increased from $700 million in 1991 to $3.6 billion for 1994.[22]

Besides increased numbers of operations, the roles performed by UN peacekeepers expanded from their original mandates of separating belligerent forces, patrolling truce lines, reporting violations, and mediating local disputes to a much more complicated series of tasks. Peacekeeping operations in the late 1980s and early 1990s have been charged with mediating the end to civil strife, monitoring elections, protecting human rights in order to make free elections possible, disarming and resettling guerrillas and their families, stopping arms traffic, administering relief operations for civilians, and making sure that democratic constitutions were written and implemented.[23] These new responsibilities assigned by the member states have raised serious challenges to the United Nations.[24]

Peace operations in the 1990s therefore are far more complex than traditional peacekeeping has been:

> It was one thing to set up peace-keeping operations without the use of force during the cold war, in order to show that conflicts between sovereign states had been suspended, whether between Syria and Israel in the Golan Heights, or between India and Pakistan in the Subcontinent. It has proved far more difficult to inject UN peace-keeping forces into active civil wars in which no government has invited them, the fighting factions are unwilling to cooperate with the UN forces, and there is little possibility of bringing political or other pressure to bear on those factions.[25]

The discouraging experiences of these new peace operations in places like Somalia, Bosnia, Western Sahara, Angola, and Rwanda have overshadowed the relative successes in Namibia, El Salvador, Cambodia, and Mozambique.[26]

A number of scholars have cautioned against undue optimism about the feasibility or desirability of multilateral interventions.[27] Ernst B. Haas, for example, argues that for the United Nations to be effective and justified in a small set of cases it must avoid the "slippery slope" that may lead it to intervene in a larger set of circumstances, particularly civil wars. He says, "I want to save the UN's legitimacy for situations that can be improved by multilateral action by preventing the organization's sliding down the slippery slope illustrated by the cases of Somalia, Bosnia, and Cambodia."[28] Stephen John Stedman details the difficulties of using UN forces to intervene in civil wars:

U.N. troops may carry international legitimacy, but internal parties will still command the asymmetries of civil war: parties win by not losing; the will of those who intervene will wane over the long term if resource and human costs run high; and intervention will be one of many commitments for outsiders, whereas the internal actors will be single-minded in their dedication.[29]

UN peacekeeping operations were designed and their operational doctrine developed to assist in the consolidation of a settlement following an interstate conflict. In the late 1980s and early 1990s, the international community attempted to stretch this instrument to serve as the mechanism to produce a settlement in cases of civil violence that result from state collapse. Not surprisingly, this extension has been problematic. The intervention in Somalia from 1992 to 1995 is a prime example of this problem.

The military operations by the United States and the United Nations in Somalia have important implications because they exemplify one of the first cases of international action in response to state collapse in the post–cold war era and because they represent experiments in new forms of multilateral peace operations. Somalia, of course, had a number of unique characteristics, and there is no single model for international actions in cases of state collapse. The Somalia intervention, however, suggests many questions and challenges that international policymakers and analysts should consider when faced with other cases of collapsed states.

2

Anatomy of State Collapse

On January 27, 1991, a popular uprising and generalized breakdown in security drove Somali president Siad Barre from his bunker in the ruins of Mogadishu into a tank that eventually took him into exile. This departure marked the formal end of a difficult era but did not usher in a new one. The Somali state, always a fragile, artificial creation dependent on external resources and suspended above a decentralized and fractious society, had collapsed. Owing in large measure to Barre's destructive, divisive policies, no broadly based political groups existed to succeed the old leader. Consequently, competing factions and anarchy filled the resulting vacuum.

With the state collapsed, the Somali people suffered the horrible brutality of living in a Hobbesian world without law or institutions to regulate relations among groups or to protect the most vulnerable from the most vicious. Violence and looting prevented economic production or the distribution of food, creating widespread famine that killed hundreds of thousands. This catastrophe came to the attention of the broad international community in mid-1992 as a complex humanitarian emergency that eventually inspired military intervention.

To understand the enormous complexity of the challenges inherent in the Somali crisis of 1992, however, one must trace the evolution of modern Somalia in light of the underlying society, economy, and culture. The Somali state, an entity defined and created by colonial powers, hovered above a predominantly pastoral, subsistence, and decentralized society. Somali culture had a complex and powerful system of ethical norms and rules to regulate behavior that was linked with the requirements of a pastoral, subsistence way of life.

The Somali pastoral system and the culture of kinship that supported it began to suffer distortions as commodity production for international

7

markets was introduced. With the arrival of colonialism Somali traditions became less connected to underlying social and cultural forces. The process of decolonization created an independent state that remained aloof from society. Following the 1969 coup that brought Siad Barre to power, and particularly after the 1977–78 war with Ethiopia, Somalia suffered under a harsh authoritarian regime that encouraged animosity among clan groups and used massive military force to put down popular protests. By 1991, when insurgents finally forced Siad Barre out of office, the Somali people faced the perils of living in the violent wreckage of a collapsed state. This deeply rooted breakdown of institutions and the interlinked deterioration of social structures and cultural constraints confronted the international community when it considered the humanitarian emergency in late 1992.

Evolution of the Fragile Somali State

Historically, subsistence-based societies such as pastoral Somalia have been common in many parts of Africa. Such social formations were characterized by the intermeshing of economic production, political life, and culture. Production, which was small in scale and coterminous with consumption, was done within the *rer* (household). Political norms and cultural values linked up with economic structures by way of the ideology of kinship, thereby creating an interlinked web of social, economic, and political institutions. As a result, an individual Somali's location in any of the three structures automatically included him or her in the others. A distinctive Somali social organization thereby emerged from the close interlinkages among the economic, cultural, and political spheres of life. This structure suited pastoral, subsistence production and allowed the Somali to survive and live with dignity in the harsh conditions of northeast Africa.

The ideology of kinship had two central elements: blood-ties and *heer*. The first was essentially a product of genealogical connections reinforced by a patrilineal system rooted in a real or invented common origin or ancestor. Somalis are divided into several major clan-families, the Saab, the Irir, and the Darod (figure 2-1). Each has its own subfamilies that further break down into numerous lineage-segments, all the way down to the *rer*. Many of the clans were geographically dispersed and often occupied noncontiguous territories (see map in front matter). Clan solidarity was maintained in part by the institution of "blood-payments"—the *diya*—whereby the lineage had collective obligations to honor certain debts and make restitution for wrongs. The clan structure was further reinforced by communal access to the range

Figure 2-1. Genealogical Chart of Somalia

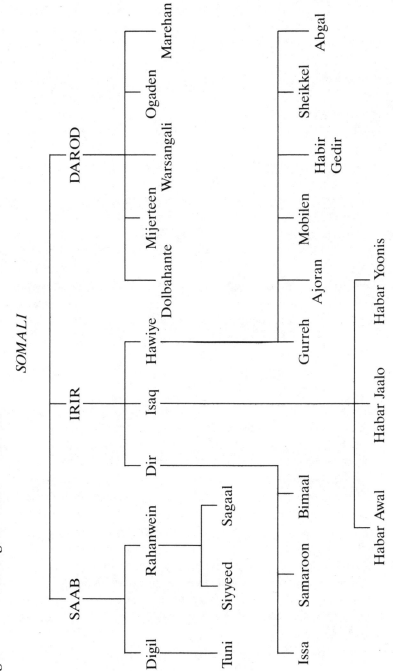

and family ownership of the herd, the principal economic asset. This acephalous society therefore was highly egalitarian and democratic as well as susceptible to frequent internecine feuds.[1]

The second aspect of kinship, *heer*, was the embodiment of common wisdom and constituted an unwritten but loosely accepted pan-Somali code of conduct. *Heer* emphasized the values of interdependence and inclusiveness and thus formed the basis for social order.[2] *Heer* did not eliminate strife but provided accepted and workable ways of dealing with disputes and conflicts. The combined meaning of these elements constituted the milieu in which the private and the public were defined.[3]

The arrival of Islam during the eighth century reinforced the inclusive dimensions of *heer*. By infusing new moral language into the culture and requiring all believers to see one another as members of a large fraternity, committed to doing and earning good in this world to secure salvation in the next life, the faith offered Somalis an additional way to expand and strengthen old models of behavior. The symbiosis of *heer* and Islam stipulated uprightness and piety, deepened meaning, and helped sharpen accepted procedures for participation in everyday living.[4] Traditional pastoral Somali economy therefore was community-oriented in its production and kin-relations and, later, Islamic principles defined the main frame of reference for political and cultural life.

Imperialism and Division

Colonialism first came to the Somali territories in a creeping fashion through trading networks.[5] As early as the tenth century, the coastal zone had been a passageway between the pastoral Somali hinterland and regional commercial centers in southeastern Africa, Egypt, coastal parts of Arabia, Persia, and even faraway China. Muslim Arabs and Persians became most successful in connecting Somalis to the world trading system and Islamic culture spread across the region. Interaction between community-based production and commodity production resulted in the emergence of formative class relations—for example, pastoral producers, *dilaals* (Somali middlemen), and merchants.[6] Some traders intermarried with Somali women, further linking Somalia to trading and cultural centers in Yemen and Oman. Somali middlemen promoted and protected transactions between foreign establishments and the pastoral society.

Trading also generated new forms of political institutionalization. As

Library Resource Center
ANATOMY OF STATE COLLAPSE
8000 NE 4th St.
Renton, WA 98056-4195

commercial coastal towns like Zeila acquired importance, a town governor was created. The objective was to bring bureaucratic structure and order into a rapidly changing cultural environment. Middle Eastern traders on the Somali coast wrote the prologue to the gradual incorporation of Somali life into the evolving regional and global systems.

But it was the onslaught of European imperialism that definitively shifted the trajectory of Somali history. Interests in India led the British to occupy the port of Aden in Yemen in 1839–40 as a strategically vital post for contact with the subcontinent. Aden's needs, particularly for meat supplies, soon brought the adjacent northern Somali coast with its abundance of sheep, goats, camels, and cattle to London's attention. By 1886, the British had signed formal agreements with representatives of some major kin groups to officially turn northern Somalia into a protectorate.

The French arrived in the region at about the same time as the British. Keen on suspected riches in Ethiopia as well as looking for a port of call on the way to Madagascar and Indochina, the French bought concessions and eventually made full claim over French Somaliland (now known as Djibouti). The Italians came next. Latecomers to the feast of partition because of their preoccupation with their own unification in the nineteenth century, the Italians were hungry for imperial grandeur. Italians descended on southern Somalia in the 1890s and formally established their colony in 1893. Although London was content to extract resources but otherwise rule indirectly in the north, Rome sent significant numbers of Italian settlers to its colony in the south, imposed a more direct administration, and eventually introduced the most brutal facets of fascism. Emperor Menilek of Ethiopia expanded his state to the east in the late nineteenth century and asserted sovereignty over the Somali-inhabited Ogaden region. Finally, British colonial authorities claimed territory inhabited by Somalis in northeastern Kenya. The Somali people therefore experienced colonialism in five separate states. Early Somali nationalists organized in opposition to this historical partition and sought to unite the five territories into a single state, Greater Somalia.

The intrusion of the powerful forces of the international market and imperialism led to the corrosion of the old Somali moral order. The end of the colonial period left Somalis with a growing divergence between the internal logic and demands of a social structure suited to a decentralized, pastoral setting, on the one hand, and the artificial, alien state and externally oriented world market system, on the other.

Decolonization and Early Independence

The postcolonial state, despite the veneer of nationalism that witnessed its birth in 1960, remained true to some of the odious characteristics of its predecessor. Many of the generation that brought independence to Somalia were men who grew up under the shadow of British and Italian colonialism. These leaders of the independence movements construed the enterprise as a rare chance to win a personally profitable place in the new structures (particularly the state) and only secondarily as an opportunity to construct new public institutions worthy of the great challenges ahead. Each segment of what was to become the power bloc (mostly traders, artisans, bureaucrats and literate- religious elements) was less concerned with the heavy structural and development questions facing Somalia and more preoccupied with gaining personal advantage.

One issue that immediately came to the fore after the inauguration of the first government in 1960 was the nature of the unification of the British and Italian Somalilands. Politicians from the south took the lion's share of positions, including the presidency, the prime ministership, more than two-thirds of the senior cabinet posts, and the two top posts in the military forces and the police. Naturally, some northerners, with some prescience, felt taken. Although many believed that leadership would be rotated between regions as promised, others felt that the whole northern region would now become a neglected outpost, especially because the northern capital of Hargeysa was nearly one thousand miles of dirt road from the capital in Mogadishu. As a result of these suspicions (and individual career grievances), a small band of young British-trained junior officers from the north attempted to take over major towns in the region in December 1961. The revolt was quickly put down. Although this episode faded away, it left behind enough embers to burn through the years.

Besides regional inequities, the political system after independence relegated to the background the interests of most Somalis as members of the regime and hangers-on made a rush for individual gains.[7] Mesmerized by the ease with which they were able to generate foreign aid to mitigate deficits and support development plans, few gave much consideration to the productive sectors of the economy or to the plight of the average Somali.[8] The state was seen as the most strategic place to insure private wealth, resulting in the creation of a multitude of political parties (political parties being one way to join the contest for regime membership). Eighteen parties took part in the first postindependence national elections of 1964 amid sharp accusations of corruption and fraud. Only three of them—the Somali Youth League (SYL), the Somali National Congress, and the Somali Democratic Union—had any national standing.[9] When the ballots were counted, the SYL emerged as the continuing majority party, with 69 out of a total of 123 seats. Soon after the new National Assembly was convened, however, 21 of the deputies from the competing parties joined the SYL as politicians sought favor from the ruling party.

A mushrooming of political parties on the eve of elections and their immediate disappearance (even after winning seats) became a peculiar characteristic of the Somali experiment with liberal democracy. The 1969 election demonstrated that this kind of political competition was symptomatic of deeper maladies. The parochialism was bewildering: more than 60 parties filed more than 1,000 candidates to vie for 122 seats. To guarantee victory, the SYL made Prime Minister Ibrahim Egal the leader of the party, transgressing established separation of power within the party. This action created the public perception that Egal and his cohort would do anything to win. The regime openly raided the national treasury (to the tune of $5 million) to buy votes and pressured the chief of the National Police Force to put his troops and logistics at the disposal of SYL party faithful.[10] Finally, electoral rules were altered from proportional representation to winner takes all—an innovation that was seen to suit the ruling "regime party" well. These factors heightened the premium put on parliamentary seats.

In this heated chase for spoils, national or local issues scarcely were debated. On the contrary, to ensure attention and have a chance of winning, each candidate identified his campaign with subclan interests. These tactics accelerated the demise of kinship and Islamic strictures and encouraged the rise of clanism. The SYL won seventy-three seats, the Somali National Congress had eleven, and the rest went to other smaller parties. When the counting was over, nearly four dozen defeated candidates challenged the results, but the Supreme Court ruled on technical grounds that it lacked any legal authority to adjudicate. With fairness and constitutionality heavily compromised, the new parliament convened. Every new deputy was set on retrieving his (all were male) campaign expenses and, therefore, to secure a favorable place in the distribution of power and privilege. The parliament was transformed into what Lewis aptly called, "a sordid marketplace," with little attention paid to the needs of the society at large.[11] After a few days of haggling, all but one member (former prime minister Abdulrazak Hussein) crossed the floor and joined the ruling SYL. Consequently, Somalia, for all practical purposes, became a one-party state. The first nine years of independent government did not create a state responsive and responsible to the challenges facing the Somali society.

Siad Barre and the Destruction of the Somali State

By 1969, it had become increasingly clear that Somali parliamentary democracy had become a travesty, an elaborate, rarefied game with little relevance to the daily challenges facing the population. On October 15, 1969, a member of the police force assassinated President Abdirashiid Ali Shermaarke. Six days later, the armed forces staged a bloodless coup. The military leaders, led by General Siad Barre and organized as the Supreme Revolutionary Council (SRC), at first received a tumultuous welcome. They were seen as heroes who had left the barracks to save the nation. The SRC had the freedom to act decisively and settle issues that the ineffective parliament had debated endlessly, such as the selection of an official orthography for the Somali language. It also acted assertively on programs of adult literacy and settlement of populations displaced by drought. In 1970 Siad Barre adopted "scientific socialism" as his regime's guiding ideology and introduced policies to outlaw clan or "tribal" identities.[12]

But this euphoria began to wane in the mid-1970s. By then it had become obvious that the SRC was not intent on restoring democracy, as promised, but would keep to itself more concentrated power and privileges, including the availability of an omnipresent secret police to discipline those deemed irreverent. Early victims of the arbitrary power included Generals Mohamed Ainanshe and Salad Gabeire, two senior coupmakers executed in 1971. Nothing exemplified the corruption of the SRC more than the actions of its chair, Siad Barre. Barre permitted state-sanctioned veneration of the "Revolution" to be twisted into a cult of personality and sycophantic flattery hitherto unseen in the history of the country.[13]

Although officially campaigning against "tribalism" and promoting scientific socialism and Greater Somalia as unifying ideologies, Siad Barre built his power by manipulating clans and implementing classic tactics of divide and rule. His regime relied heavily on support from the Darod clan, especially the Marehan, Dolbahante, and Ogaden subclans.

The war with Ethiopia (1977–78) revealed Siad Barre's weaknesses and hollow authority. Political leaders in Mogadishu had insisted long before independence, on the right of self-determination for Somalis living in the Ogaden region of Ethiopia, and skirmishes and support for the insurgents in Ethiopia marked relations between Somalia and Ethiopia, in the 1960s and early 1970s.[14] In 1977, Barre sent his troops, believing that seizing the Ogaden was within his reach because of Ethiopia's postrevolutionary weakness and Somalia's well-equipped military (thanks to generous Soviet support). The Somalis quickly made deep advances and threatened the key towns of Harar and Dire Dawa. The Ethiopian military, resupplied by the Soviets and supported by Cuban troops, counterattacked and pushed the Somali forces back across the border.

The defeat removed pan-Somali nationalism as a legitimating ideology for Siad Barre's regime. The Ogaden debacle also led to a search for clan scapegoats, and clan cleavages burst into the open.[15] The regime's use of clan rivalries and patronage, on the one hand, and repression, on the other, to maintain authority became increasingly clear in the 1980s. As Barre's power eroded, his reliance on arbitrary force grew until by the 1980s he relied upon little but terror and manipulations of clan identities to remain in power.

Economic Collapse

The Somali economy reached a crisis at the same time that politics had descended into a violent struggle for power. The two dynamics amplified each other. The economy had always been precarious and dependent on the vagaries of pastoral and peasant production. Until mid-1988, livestock represented well over 80 percent of the goods exported. But the returns to producers were meager. Government expenditures for this dominant component of the rural sector went from 3 percent in 1963 to 14 percent in 1986–87.[16] Most of these allocations were spent on improvements of marketing facilities. The neglect of peasant farming was greater, making Somalia the sub-Saharan country most dependent on imported food.[17]

The 1980s also brought a change in prices as stiff competition for the Saudi market (which accounted for more than 90 percent of Somali exports) from countries like Australia cut deeply into what had been nearly a Somali monopoly. The decline in oil prices, the internationalization of the livestock market, and the anxiety of the Somali state about the possibility of losing such a critical market led to a sharp decline of export prices. This in turn severely affected state revenues and producer incomes. Table 2-1 illustrates the decline in export prices for livestock pre- and post-1985.

Table 2-1. Somalia: Livestock Export Prices
Dollars per head unless noted otherwise

Item	Pre-January 1985	Post-January 1985	Percent change
Sheep	53	42	− 21.75
Cattle	280	213	− 23.95
Camels	450	390	− 11.11

Source: Adapted from Abdi Samatar, "Social Classes and Economic Restructuring in Pastoral Africa: Notes from Somalia." *African Studies Review*, vol. 35 (April 1992), p. 112. Livestock exports have not changed much as of December 1990. However, since mid-1988 the quantity declined precipitously, and livestock became second to the hardly robust export of bananas.

The fall of prices and the lack of growth in the quantity of animals exported (livestock exports reached their peak in 1972) created hard times for most people.[18] This situation meant diminishing terms of trade for producers, fewer profits for most merchants, and shrinking foreign exchange for the state.[19] Pastoral producers faced the greatest pressures. Despite the fact that pastoralists possessed deep and effective knowledge that allowed them to survive in the extremely harsh Somali terrain, market volatility turned pastoral living into an increasingly precarious undertaking.[20]

Besides having to deal with poor opportunities on the international commodity markets, Somalia faced the burdens that come with the interventions of the international financial institutions such as the International Monetary Fund (IMF) and World Bank, and the debilitating weight of debt. Negative balance of payment (the consequence of declining revenues and unwise spending), poor production, and a high rate of population growth (about 3.1 percent), drove the Somali state to look for external transfusions of resources.[21] The IMF and the World Bank facilitated this borrowing by exacting a heavy conditionality.

The first Structural Adjustment Program (SAP) was promulgated in 1981. As part of the agreement, the regime opened the door for Italian investors who had their eyes on the banana industry, which was originally started by the fascists and dominated by Italian capital even during the heyday of statism. As liberalization brought some growth in a stagnating sector, Abdi Samatar writes, "The greatest beneficiaries of the recent boom in the banana industry are the Italian multinational investor (De Nadai, the sole exporter of Somali bananas and the only importer of agricultural inputs), the importing countries of the Middle-East and Italy, and . . . the plantation owners."[22] De Nadai's total grip and domination of the Somali banana industry were accompanied by peculiar, sectorwide forms of child labor. Other consequences of Somalia's economic crisis included inflation (between 500 percent and 800 percent annually), decay or complete disappearance of social services (including education), and sky-rocketing unemployment.[23]

Somalia had established the ability to attract relatively large amounts of aid, in per capita terms and as a percentage of GNP (the latter hovered around 25 percent).[24] Despite these high levels, Somali indebtedness was egregious. The country had the unenviable distinction of having one of the highest debt-to-GNP ratios in the continent—nearly 203 percent, which translates into a debt per capita figure of more than $350. This figure is incomprehensible in a country with a GNP per capita of less than $175.[25]

Repression and Resistance

In April 1978, immediately after the Ogaden war, a poorly organized and parochial coup attempt led by Mijerteen colonels failed. In a pattern that would be repeated against other opponents, the regime launched vicious, communal reprisals against the Mijerteen clan. Civilians were targeted, and communal economic structures such as water wells and livestock destroyed. Militias from rival clans received arms and were encouraged to seize Mijerteen property.

As a result, many Mijerteen fled into exile, where some joined armed opposition groups that later merged to become the Somali Democratic Salvation Front (SSDF). Among those who fled was Colonel Abdullahi Yusuf, one of the few surviving plotters of the 1978 coup attempt. Under his leadership, the SSDF operated as a multiclan front for a short time but soon fell prey to factionalism and became a Mijerteen-based movement.[26] Cooperation with Ethiopia provided bases of operation and resources but reduced the SSDF's ability to win popular support and the organization was moribund by the late 1980s.

The pattern of abuse targeted against specific clans was repeated with greater ruthlessness and devastation in the north. Following the 1978 Somali defeat against Ethiopia, many Ogadenis sympathetic to Siad Barre moved into lands traditionally occupied by Isaqs, sparking intense clan antagonisms in the north. Northern opposition grew further in response to the failing economy, the collapse of political legitimacy, and premeditated repression, reawakening long-suppressed discontent over regional disparity. In 1981, intellectuals, businessmen, *sheikhs*, former military officers, disgruntled cabinet ministers, and diplomats with varying ideologies largely from the northern Isaq clan formed the Somali National Movement (SNM). The leaders announced their commitment to overthrow Siad Barre's regime by the force of arms.[27]

The SNM, like the SSDF, operated from bases in Ethiopia but had little presence in Somalia for most of the 1980s. In April 1988 the governments in Mogadishu and Addis Ababa, both challenged by growing insurgencies and anxious to free up forces guarding their border, signed a treaty of nonaggression and noninterference.[28] The Ethiopian regime further agreed to close opposition military bases, thereby forcing the SNM to change its strategy quickly. The SNM decided to launch a "last chance" offensive and fight its way into northern Somalia, particularly the Hargeysa, Berbera, and Burao triangle inhabited mostly by Isaq communities.

The result was a bloodbath. SNM fighters quickly overran many villages until they captured Burao and moved into Hargeysa in May 1989. The regime, at first caught off-guard, responded by sending its full military might under the command of Siad Barre's son-in-law General Mohammed Siad Hersi "Morgan." The battles were fierce and brutal. Hargeysa suffered unrestricted aerial bombardment (some planes were piloted by South African mercenaries) and heavy artillery fire. Within days, the second largest city of Somalia lay in ruins (more than 70 percent destroyed), and many of its citizens fled across the border to Ethiopia.[29] The regime unleashed loyal Ogadeni militias, once armed to fight Ethiopians, to attack the civilian Isaq population.[30] Other, non-Isaq northern clans also received arms. Subsequently, most of northern Somalia became a lawless territory, a region in which the central state apparatus had collapsed. The regime regained control (until the end of January 1991) over the destroyed cities and continued to terrorize what was left of the urban areas, while the SNM roamed the countryside.[31]

With the state disintegrating in the north and central regions, chaos and interclan fighting spread steadily to the south. In early 1989 the Somali Patriotic Movement (SPM) appeared in southern Somalia. Members of this group, essentially from the Ogaden lineage, had previously been part of the Somali armed forces and bureaucracy.[32] Their immediate disaffection was linked to the demotion and subsequent arrest of Minister of Defence General Gabyo who was the highest ranking Ogadeni during the mid- and late 1980s. Armed SPM clashes with the regime started in earnest in Afmadu in March 1989. These actions underscored the fact that insurgent activity now covered some parts of middle and lower Juba and Banaadir.

The Hawiye clan became the next focus of the regime's ruthlessness. In 1989 a mutiny by Hawiye troops in Galcayo brought the now familiar reaction in the form of communal punishments. The Hawiye-led United Somali Congress (USC) had been set up in 1987 in Rome by some Hawiye who had been members of the SNM. The USC suffered divisions from the start as some Hawiye, including General Mohamed Farah Aideed, chose to continue working with the SNM for a time.

The spreading of resistance to southern Somalia, as civil strife assumed national proportions, generated the forces that eroded state institutions and led to its complete collapse in 1991. As Siad Barre's government controlled less and less of the countryside, Somalis sought the safety and protection of their lineages and subclans.[33] With the livestock trading economic base severely disrupted by conflict in the north and the productive agricultural areas of southern Somalia sliding into violent anarchy, the financial basis of state and local institutions eroded.

Nearly all facets of Somali political life had become divided along clan lines, with actions analyzed with a view to the clan affiliation of the relevant actors.[34] Barre's regime long had been regarded as an institution captured by one set of clan interests. Eventually, nearly all of Barre's most sensitive appointments came from his immediate blood relations and others related through marriage.[35] By 1990 the national army had become predominantly Marehan and was viewed by most Somalis as a threat.

Opposition to Siad Barre's manipulation of clan affinities ironically took the form of clan-based insurgencies.[36] The regime's practice of targeting clans for punishment pushed Somalis to organize opposition along clan lines and in defense of the clan. Barre's tactic thereby made cooperation among opposition groups more difficult by making divisive clan identity the principal focus of organization. According to Hussein Adam, "The armed opposition groups adopted the short-run policy of utilizing clan-recruited volunteers to combat Barre's state-manipulated clanism."[37] Numerous attempts to create broad-based fronts or to at least forge cooperation among clan-based organizations failed.[38]

Endgame in Mogadishu

While Siad Barre's forces terrorized much of the countryside in the waning months of the 1980s, unrest in Mogadishu increased in response to economic collapse and mounting human rights abuses. Aroused by sermons from the *Ulema* during Friday prayers, the people of Mogadishu came out on the streets in protest on July 14, 1989. Troops were called out and a violent clash ensued. Mogadishu's municipal authorities reported several soldiers and twenty-three civilians killed, with fifty-nine wounded. However, eyewitness and unofficial sources have put the civilian death toll much higher.[39] Politically motivated arrests and executions furthered the sense of terror. According to Amnesty International, "[Among] those detained included 46 people from the Medina district of Moqdishu, mostly members of the Issaq clan, picked out because of their clan origin, who were arrested on 16 July [1989] and executed extrajudicially that night by soldiers on a beach at Jezira, 30 kilometers southwest of Moqdishu."[40]

The regime's slaughtering of civilians continued unabated in the countryside as well. Amnesty International reported the killing of about 120 civilians near Galcayo, in central Somalia, on November 24, 1989, and another 100 unarmed villagers in Belet Weyn. These incidents were part of a deadly policy to punish communities in areas seen as supporters of mutinous units of the army or opposition forces operating in these localities.[41]

Siad Barre's regime had collapsed, and his "national" army had become merely a personal militia. The *Washington Post* reported the following from Mogadishu nearly a year before Siad Barre's flight:

> The 20-year rule of Somali leader Mohamed Siad Barre appears to be crumbling. . . . [T]he octogenarian ruler is unable to control the nation's armed forces, which are accused of committing recent mass murders of civilians in central Somalia and numerous acts of banditry, looting and harassment....[The Presidential Guards are] the prime suspects in increasing numbers of rapes and robberies of civilians and foreign aid warehouses.[42]

In April 1990 a group composed of prestigious figures and perceived to be politically moderate, including Aden Abdulla Osman, Somalia's first president, published a manifesto. This document called for the formation of a provisional government and political reconciliation with the various insurgent groups. Siad Barre arrested most of the signatories (the so-called Manifesto Group). Although it included figures from several clans, the Manifesto Group came to be seen as a largely Hawiye and Mogadishu-based organization.[43]

By mid-1990, public demonstrations, riots, and looting in Mogadishu mounted, and arrests and repression increased. Armed, clan-based opposition movements began to coordinate their actions. Barre became a prisoner in his own compound with control over only a small enclave in the capital. Some labeled him the mayor of Mogadishu.[44] The Somali national army had long since collapsed into clan-based factions, and only a small group of Marehan remained loyal to the "president." In a real sense, Siad Barre ended his reign as the first regional warlord of the 1990s.[45]

On January 27, 1991, amidst the carnage, Siad Barre's twenty-one year military and personal dictatorship came to an end. Barre and remnants of his supporters left Mogadishu in a military convoy headed for the safety of his kinsmen in the Gedo region.[46] As soon as the detested center collapsed, a new vicious jostling for individual and clanistic power commenced, exacerbated by revenge-seeking rage (particularly against the Marehan and other Darod communities perceived to be the supporters of Siad Barre). An orgy of looting (partly by Barre's fleeing troops) of public and private property erupted, which culminated in anarchy and chaos in most major urban centers. For many thousands of the inhabitants of Mogadishu and other areas in southern Somalia, living became a nightmare as more and more of them were terrorized by armed gangs.

Anarchy

The complete collapse of the Somali state following Siad Barre's overthrow in January 1991 created a vacuum of legitimate institutions that was filled in different ways in different regions. Lawlessness, anarchy, and the consequent famine were most profound in southern Somalia, especially in the area between the Juba and Shebele rivers, and in the capital of Mogadishu (see map in front matter), where no single group proved dominant. In central or northeastern Somalia, the Somali Salvation Democratic Front (SSDF) had more support (or at least fewer competitors) and achieved a kind of rough stability that limited looting and prevented widespread famine. In northwestern Somalia, the Somali National Movement (SNM) gained control and proclaimed the former British colony the independent Somaliland Republic. The SNM continued to insist on independence despite lack of international recognition.

The most dramatic violence and the source of the images that later came to international attention occurred in the area between Kismayu, Mogadishu, and Belet Weyn. In this triangle, violence took place on two levels. The primary conflict was between militias, pitting clan and subclans organized in rival organizations against one another for control of territory and resources.

Beneath this factional strife was looting and banditry carried out by armed teenage gangs known as *mooryaan*. These gangs terrorized the countryside and urban areas in the infamous "technicals" (generally vehicles mounted with heavy guns). They were primarily motivated by the desire to gain access to war booty and were beholden to no group politically.[47]

Following the ouster of Siad Barre, members of his immediate clan, the Marehan, and some from the larger clan-family, the Darod, fled south across the Juba river, where they regrouped in the traditional Darod territory from Kismayu upriver to Bardera and on to the Ethiopian border. Meanwhile, the Hawiye-based United Somali Congress took control of Mogadishu and regions north of the capital where they have traditionally been predominant. In early 1991, the USC and various factions of the Darod fought a series of skirmishes on a long and shifting front extending from Mogadishu to Kismayu to central Somalia. In April 1991, Barre's forces fighting alongside the Marehan-based Somali National Front (SNF) advanced to the outskirts of Mogadishu, causing USC forces under the leadership of General Mohamed Farah Aideed to launch a counteroffensive.

As Siad Barre retreated, his armed men practiced a classic scorched earth campaign, destroying the crops, animals, and homes of the unarmed civilians along the way. Caught in the middle were the large but politically powerless and poorly armed agricultural communities of the Rahanwin, Digil, Gosha, and others. These communities, as well as the ethnically distinct Banadir coastal town dwellers, were devastated by looting, rape, and massacres during periods of military occupation by various factions. As a result, the agricultural heartland of Somalia was destroyed and hundreds of thousands of Somalis fled to Kenya, Ethiopia, or to urban areas in an often futile search for security.[48]

In the days following Siad Barre's flight from Mogadishu, Ali Mahdi Mohamed, the leader of the USC faction associated with the Manifesto Group, proclaimed himself interim president and began appointing a cabinet. His rival in the USC, General Mohamed Farah Aideed, and other factional leaders rejected Ali Mahdi's leadership. The threat posed by Siad Barre's troops postponed the showdown within the USC until late 1991 when destructive battles broke out in Mogadishu. This conflict was a confused mixture of competition between factions of the USC, a personal leadership struggle between Aideed and Ali Mahdi, a fight between two subclans, the Habir Gedir and Abgal, and a desperate struggle to win public office and the financial benefits such positions promised.

In the course of the fighting, looting became all encompassing—not only were homes looted of their furnishings but also their door frames, wiring, pipes, and structural steel. Nearly all public infrastructure, from bridges to power and water lines, was blown up or dug out.[49] Eventually a "Green Line" divided the two factions. Ali Mahdi's Abgal-based militia was confined to the north of Mogadishu while Aideed's Habir Gedir forces controlled the south, including areas around the critical airport and seaport. Several attempts by neutral clan elders to mediate a cease-fire in late 1991 failed.[50]

Besides the fighting within Mogadishu, factions fought one another in complex battles across southern Somalia. The key southern city of Kismayu changed hands a number of times in 1991 and 1992 as one faction of the Ogadeni Somali Patriotic Movement led by Colonel Omar Jess fought with another faction led by General Morgan. Heavy fighting also took place at Bardera. As a result of all these factional fights, hundreds of thousands of civilians were at risk of starvation.

Northern Somalia did not escape the fall-out from the defeat of Siad Barre's regime. Once the center folded, provincial authorities immediately gave up or were quickly overwhelmed. The Somali National Movement (SNM), the insurgent force that had fought most tenaciously against Siad Barre in the 1980s and paid the highest price in return, defined itself as the new and rightful power in northern Somalia. Soon, the SNM's armed wing began to intimidate non-Isaq areas and pressure them into accepting SNM political authority. Battles and skirmishes were fought in several localities. In the end, the SNM achieved at least acquiescence from most residents of northern Somalia. In May 1991, with its dominance established and the south in complete disarray, the SNM's leadership declared the independence of the north (the old British Somaliland) as the new Somaliland Republic.

As the situation crystallized, many Somalis were shocked by the SNM's failure to lead the whole country toward a new political order. Some perceived in the SNM's rejection of the south the betrayal of the principles that had been articulated during years of fighting to liberate the Somali people as a whole. These critics now believed that the SNM was essentially another clanistic and secessionist group. The SNM's actions contributed to the dissolution of Somalia as a nation-state, the destruction of pan-Somalism, and the acceleration of the balkanization of northeast Africa.[51]

Others, however, suggest that the independence declaration reflected a broadly based popular rejection of southern Somali politics that SNM leaders could not ignore. The long-simmering resentments over regional disparities dating back to the early independence period, the perception that many southern-based clans remained unmoved and silent while the Isaq faced Siad Barre's military repression in 1988, and a sense that isolating the north from the chaos and violence of the south best protected the region provided a rationale for rejecting a pan-Somali political agenda, for the time being at least.[52]

Conclusion

The tragic images broadcast by the Western media in mid-1992 captured the horrible degenerative stages of a long process of political, social, and economic disintegration in Somalia. A decentralized, pastoral society with a culture based on kinship and Islam became distorted under colonialism by the penetration of market relations and artificial state structures. Decolonization and the institutions of the early independence years failed to establish effective new ways to connect Somali society to the state. Siad Barre's regime became increasingly authoritarian over time and in the end relied upon brute force and the manipulation of clan animosities to remain in power. Opposition groups failed to develop an agenda beyond the need to remove Barre. When the state finally collapsed, it left behind little but the wreckage of distorted traditions and artificial institutions, a vacuum that the most ruthless elements in the society soon filled. A long and complex process led to the collapse of the Somali state, compelling the international community to consider what it could do to reverse the deterioration.

3

Missed Opportunities and the Decision to Intervene

The humanitarian catastrophe in southern Somalia that reached international attention in late 1992 did not arise overnight. Observers had documented and analyzed the growing debilitation of political institutions in Somalia in the late 1980s and early 1990s in great detail.[1] International actors, most notably the United States, that had maintained a significant economic and military assistance relationship until the late 1980s, recognized the warning signs of disaster but lacked the interest and the strategy to act effectively. Left on its own, the Somali political system collapsed into anarchy. Even a semblance of government ended with Siad Barre's overthrow in January 1991.

In mid-1991, regional actors attempted to convene peace conferences in Djibouti to forge a new ruling coalition with little success. The United Nations finally took action to respond to the political vacuum in early 1992 and succeeded in getting the major factional leaders in Mogadishu to sign a cease-fire in March. The United Nations and the rest of the international community, however, responded slowly to the opportunity to broaden the cease-fire into an effective process to promote political reconciliation and institutional rehabilitation. Lawlessness and the consequent famine and humanitarian emergency led the United States to sponsor an airlift of relief supplies and the United Nations to send peacekeepers. By November 1992, however, the underlying challenges of state collapse remained and spurred public pressures for more effective actions. President George Bush responded with the decision to send U.S. forces to lead an international intervention.

It is too facile to argue that certain actions at any one moment would necessarily have prevented the collapse of Somalia, but in hindsight one can make the case that creative and concerted attention by external actors with some leverage and resources would have helped. The resources necessary to discourage collapse were far less extensive than what was required to assist in reassembling a viable order once anarchy was unleashed. Thus we begin our consideration of international options for intervention by discussing opportunities to prevent state collapse that the international community missed.

Encouraging Political Transition

During the cold war, first the Soviet Union and then the United States provided large quantities of assistance to Somalia, principally in the form of military aid and financial resources channeled through the central authorities in Mogadishu. Both superpowers provided such patronage in an effort to check the other's ambitions in the Horn of Africa region and in exchange for access to military facilities.[2] From 1983 to 1990, the United States committed almost $500 million worth of military resources to Somalia.[3] Italian government and businesses also had sizable financial interests in Somalia, some of them tied to political corruption.[4] Much of the economic aid went to reward the president's allies, little to sustainable development projects.[5] Washington supported the increasingly authoritarian regime until congressional pressures forced a suspension in 1988.[6]

Despite this involvement in Somali affairs in the late 1970s and 1980s, the United States and most of the rest of the world watched the violent endgame and the unraveling of Siad Barre's regime without forming even the beginnings of a coordinated strategy to promote a peaceful transition. With the cold war waning, it seemed to be in no state's interest to care about the growing chaos in a remote corner of northeast Africa. As a result, the international community missed a series of clear opportunities to encourage and pressure Siad Barre to step down and begin the transition to a new order before violence and internecine bloodletting led to the complete destruction of state institutions. Probably no single action would have removed Barre. Concerted diplomatic initiatives at a relatively modest cost in the late 1980s, however, could have prevented the chaos and humanitarian crisis that precipitated the costly military intervention in late 1992. Ambassador Mohamed Sahnoun, the UN special representative in 1992, puts the proposition assertively: "If the international community had intervened earlier and more effectively in Somalia, much of the catastrophe that has unfolded could have been avoided."[7]

One early opportunity followed the massacres in northern Somalia in April–June 1988 (detailed in chapter 2). The Department of State hired a consultant, Robert Gersony, to tour the region and report on conditions. Gersony's message was unambiguous:

> In response to the SNM's [Somali National Movement's] May 1988 intensification of the civil conflict in northern Somalia, the Somali Armed Forces appears to have engaged in a widespread, systematic and extremely violent assault on the unarmed civilian Issak population of northern Somalia in places where and at times when neither resistance to these actions nor danger to the Somali Armed Forces was present. The Somali Armed Forces conducted what appears to be a systematic pattern of attacks against unarmed, civilian Issak villages, watering points and grazing areas of northern Somalia, killing many of their residents and forcing the survivors to flee for safety to remote areas within Somalia or to other countries. . . . In an additional pattern of systematic, organized and sustained Somali Armed Forces actions in Berbera, which has not been the object of an SNM attack or the scene of a conflicts, at least five hundred, and perhaps many more Issak men were systematically rounded up and murdered, mainly by having their throats cut, and then buried in mass graves, during the four months following the intensification of the conflict, apparently solely because they were Issaks.[8]

This catastrophe should have served as an unmistakable alarm and compelling early warning signal to the international community that Siad Barre's political machine had deteriorated into armed violence against its civilian population.

It is plausible to argue that external patrons, most notably the United States and Italy, maintained sufficient leverage over the regime in Mogadishu in 1988 so that a well-coordinated diplomatic initiative might have facilitated a mediated end to the civil war before destruction spread further.[9] Regional states such as Ethiopia and Djibouti maintained contacts with elements of the opposition and could have assisted an international effort. U.S. Ambassador Frank Crigler, in fact, began making statements that urged Siad Barre to seek reconciliation in 1989. His efforts, however, were undercut by continued U.S. military assistance and joint training exercises.[10] Other donors did not join in coordinated pressure. By late 1989, following the riots and massacres in Mogadishu, Crigler recognized that the use of assistance to encourage reform had failed. He abandoned his diplomatic initiative and began reducing U.S. personnel in Mogadishu in anticipation of the coming troubles.[11]

Another missed opportunity occurred in May 1990 when the Manifesto Group made its opposition and willingness to challenge Siad Barre public. By this time the international community had overwhelming evidence that, unless something was done, a violent transition was on the horizon.[12] Secretary of State James Baker reportedly told the Somali prime minister that U.S. bilateral assistance would be suspended unless the government improved its respect for human rights.[13] There was no concerted international effort to pressure Siad Barre to step down or to assist the Manifesto Group or any other opposition group to remove him.[14] As in 1988 following the bombing of Hargeysa, the international community had the information it needed but lacked the will or institutionalized mechanism to act. This second lost opportunity made the collapse of the state with all the consequent costs for Somalia and the world difficult to avoid.

At this late date a number of international actors attempted to hold talks among the opposition movements and create a coalition that could move into the vacuum as Siad Barre's power evaporated. Italy tried to start mediation between the Manifesto Group and Siad Barre's government in mid-1990 without success.[15] Rome encouraged Egyptian Minister of Foreign Affairs Boutros Boutros-Ghali to hold last-minute talks between Siad Barre and the opposition in Cairo in December 1990, but several opposition movements, most notably the Somali National Movement (SNM) and United Somali Congress (USC), refused to talk with Barre.[16] As late as January 1991 Italy reportedly was encouraging a settlement that would have allowed Barre to remain as interim head of state.[17]

In a tragic unfolding of events, chaos and insecurity built up until Siad Barre was forced out of Mogadishu. The uncontrolled street violence in the capital led nearly all embassies, international organizations, and nongovernmental organizations to close their offices. During the night and early morning of January 5–6, 1991, lawlessness and violence led to a daring helicopter rescue of U.S. and other diplomatic officials from the U.S. embassy.[18] According to T. Frank Crigler, former U.S. ambassador to Somalia, the United States "turned out the lights, closed the door, and forgot about the place."[19] On January 27, Siad Barre finally fled in a tank toward his home area of Gedo, leaving Mogadishu in ruins.

Limiting State Collapse

As detailed in chapter 2, Somali opposition movements lacked the institutional bases and political vision to cooperate once Siad Barre had been overthrown. The government of Djibouti, with the support of Egypt, Italy, and other regional states, held two conferences in June and July 1991 in a further attempt to end the fighting among the insurgent groups struggling for dominance after Siad Barre's downfall. The chaotic nature of the Somali factions and the rivalries among them hindered the search for a solution. Mohamed Farah Aideed declined to attend so long as Ali Mahdi—his rival in the United Somali Congress and in Mogadishu—claimed to be interim president. The Somali Patriotic Movement participated but later repudiated its representative, and the SNM refused to attend, arguing that it no longer sought a role in Somalia since its May declaration of independence. Many Somalis regarded the Djibouti talks as an Italian attempt to move its new allies in the Manifesto Group, including Ali Mahdi, into the positions recently vacated by their old ally, Siad Barre.[20]

These various uncoordinated attempts to find a political settlement failed for several reasons. The international community acted late, proposing talks on power sharing, for example, when the opposition was on the verge of victory and no longer interested in compromise. Each attempt was an improvisation, with the inevitable delays, contradictions, and mixed messages that weakened the efforts.[21] No institutionalized mechanism existed in the international community to act effectively once evidence of impending state collapse mounted. One analyst believes that in mid-1991, "If the UN had given its full support to the Djibouti conference or had taken up the matter in the General Assembly, success, even if partial, might have been possible."[22] Siad Barre's collapse coincided with several other international events, from the ending of the cold war to the conflict with Iraq, that altered how great powers viewed the Horn of Africa. In these circumstances, the international community's "heart was not in" efforts to assist the transition in Somalia, according to Italy's ambassador.[23] Throughout 1991, the international community, ignoring political reconciliation, largely left Somalia to nongovernmental organizations who provided humanitarian assistance.

Early UN Actions

As lawlessness and banditry escalated, a complex humanitarian emergency of massive proportions developed and eventually forced international attention to Somalia. As detailed in chapter 2, the collapse of the state, especially in southern Somalia, and the subsequent looting, factional fighting, and consequent displacement of civilians and disruption of economic activity unleashed a famine that put some 330,000 at imminent risk of death.[24]

Andrew Natsios, the head of the U.S. Agency for International Development's Office of Foreign Disaster Assistance, testified before Congress in late January 1992 that Somalia was "the greatest humanitarian emergency in the world."[25]

The Security Council acted in January by invoking Chapter VII of the UN Charter and imposing an arms embargo. The resolution found a threat to international peace based on predominantly internal conditions. The United Nations stated that it was "gravely alarmed at the rapid deterioration of the situation in Somalia and the heavy loss of human life and widespread material damage resulting from the conflict in the country and aware of its consequences on the stability and peace in the region."[26] At the same time Natsios was making his statement, the U.S. mission to the United Nations, fearing the financial obligations of growing peacekeeping budgets, insisted on watering down Resolution 733 so that it did not call for peacekeeping.[27]

The United Nations' first significant steps to encourage political reconciliation took place more than a year after Siad Barre's downfall. The secretary general invited representatives of Ali Mahdi and Mohamed Farah Aideed, the United Somali Congress factional leaders who controlled sections of Mogadishu, to New York in February 1992, where they signed a vague cease-fire. UN Special Envoy James Jonah mediated an additional cease-fire document signed by the two on March 3, 1992 in Mogadishu. The United Nations concentrated in the peace talks on the factions in the capital generating most of the fighting, thereby marginalizing those leaders and clans—such as the Murasade and Hawadle—that had remained neutral.[28]

The March 1992 cease-fire provided a breathing space for political negotiations, but the international community failed to exploit this opportunity. As one sharp critic put it, "After the cessation of hostilities U.N. senior diplomats foundered in the field, the Security Council dithered, and U.N. relief agencies squandered valuable time."[29] The Security Council decided on April 24 (six weeks after the agreement) to establish a UN Operation in Somalia (UNOSOM, later labeled UNOSOM I) to monitor the cease-fire and supported a ninety-day plan of action for emergency humanitarian assistance. Pursuant to Resolution 751 (April 1992), the United Nations sent 50 unarmed monitors to Mogadishu and agreed in principle to deploy a 500-member security force to escort humanitarian deliveries. Again at U.S. insistence, the Security Council postponed plans to send peacekeeping forces.[30] The secretary general appointed Ambassador Mohamed Sahnoun of Algeria his special representative for Somalia and Brigadier General Imtiaz Shaheen of Pakistan chief military observer.[31]

International policymakers, however, focused primarily on the cease-fire as a means to facilitate humanitarian operations rather than as the first step in a broader strategy to promote political reconciliation to fill the underlying vacuum of authority.[32] The emphasis on cease-fire, while necessary as a precondition for humanitarian operations, also had the effect of promoting militia leaders as the primary political actors. A creative diplomatic initiative supported by joint UN-Somali operations to set up and enforce zones of peace and channels for food relief along with other confidence-building measures may have created a framework for broader political reconciliation to begin in March 1992. By missing this opportunity and allowing tensions to fester and conflicts to flare, the crisis in Somalia became a catastrophe, divisions widened, and the costs of reconciliation rose. Somali leaders may have been able to accept a negotiated settlement in March 1992 that they could not accept in March 1993 because the intervening violence raised the stakes, weakened civilian leaders, and strengthened the most ruthless factions.

The United States Responds

The crisis remained largely beyond the Western public purview until mid-1992.[33] Disturbing images of mass starvation, coupled with extensive documentation of the diversion of international relief by armed factions and bandits, generated increased public pressure in the West for more effective action. A July 1992 front-page story from Baidoa with accompanying photo in the New York Times focused attention and led other media to pursue the story.[34] Editorials with titles like "The Hell Called Somalia" appeared in leading newspapers.[35] Visits by a number of prominent individuals, from Irish president Mary Robinson to United Nations' Children's Fund (UNICEF) spokesperson Audrey Hepburn provided the focal points or "hooks" for media coverage. In Washington, the House Select Committee on Hunger, as well as Senators Nancy Kassebaum (who traveled to Somalia in July 1992) and Paul Simon, drew further attention to the crisis.[36]

With the cease-fire eroding and banditry rising, relief supplies could not get to the famine zone in southern Somalia. Major international nongovernmental organizations, most notably the International Committee of the Red Cross and the U.S.-based CARE, lobbied aggressively for greater international involvement. Boutros-Ghali, frustrated with his inability to get the United Nations to take the kind of forceful action he thought justified, complained publicly that the West was more interested in the "rich man's war" in Bosnia than the Somali catastrophe.[37]

These pressures finally led to a response from Washington in August 1992. President George Bush announced that he would assign U.S. military aircraft to transport food relief, ostensibly to speed up deliveries to remote towns in the interior and circumvent Mogadishu's bandit-infested harbor. Neither this initiative nor a parallel attempt to auction some food relief to merchants in Mogadishu at reduced prices succeeded in overcoming the fundamental problem of insecurity and looting.[38] Although the airlift provided needed food, the policy failed to recognize the political challenges state collapse posed. Looters captured much of the relief, and conflict worsened around Bardhere, for example, as militias fought for the valuable supplies.[39] The problem was never predominantly insufficient food but the absence of political authority and security for civil society to operate.

Through much of late 1992, diplomatic efforts to broker an end to the Somali impasse failed. Special Representative Mohamed Sahnoun tried to mediate cease-fires among the armed factions in a painstaking series of talks. Sahnoun won considerable respect from a broad array of Somalis and other observers by demonstrating the patience to listen respectfully to their concerns and aspirations. After several difficult bargaining sessions, Sahnoun succeeded in finalizing an agreement on August 12, to deploy the 500-member security force authorized in UN Resolution 751, adopted in April 1992.

Despite this success and what some saw as momentum toward political settlement, Sahnoun was forced to resign in October 1992. In his resignation he blamed his "bitter experiences with the U.N. bureaucracy" and complained that he did not have the "mandate to deploy more troops and that is why the humanitarian activities are failing."[40] Boutros-Ghali objected to Sahnoun's statements to the media criticizing the United Nations. The secretary general named Ismat Kittani, an Iraqi diplomat, to replace Sahnoun.

The UN troops placed in Mogadishu in September 1992, known as UNOSOM I, consisted of 500 lightly armed Pakistanis. This force operated under a traditional UN peacekeeping mandate that required strict neutrality and the consent of local parties prior to deployment.[41] Aideed's forces occupied the areas around the airport and port and wanted to maintain control of these strategic assets in order to capture the benefits of relief shipments.

As a result, Aideed refused to allow the Pakistanis to deploy effectively, and he restricted them to their barracks. UNOSOM I lacked the mandate to challenge local militia leaders, and the Pakistanis had neither the weapons nor the rules of engagement to effectively enforce UN policy.[42]

By November 1992, UN humanitarian activities, even when bolstered by the U.S. airlift and the presence of 500 peacekeeping troops, seemed incapable of managing the catastrophe, and calls for more forceful action grew. The scale of the disaster was extraordinary. The U.S. Centers for Disease Control and Prevention verified that mortality rights were "among the highest ever documented by a population survey among famine-affected civilians."[43] One informed specialist estimated that of a total population of fewer than 6 million, 350,000 Somalis perished from malnutrition and associated diseases in 1992 while nearly 1 million fled into refugee camps.[44]

The inability of ad hoc humanitarian and diplomatic initiatives to reduce the vicious spiral of violence and suffering in Somalia led the United Nations to consolidate its initiatives in UNOSOM I. Under Sahnoun, an agreement for the deployment of 500 peacekeepers eventually was reached with the militia leaders in Mogadishu. The looting and insecurity, however, limited humanitarian operations and prevented movement on political reconciliation and state rehabilitation. By November, the UNOSOM I strategy of using a symbolic military force to encourage negotiations among powerful militias seemed unable to produce results. Without a political settlement and security, the humanitarian catastrophe would continue.

Bush's Decision to Intervene

In Washington, the National Security Council's deputies committee met on November 21, 1992, to consider options. Although Chairman of the Joint Chiefs of Staff Colin Powell and others in the Department of Defense earlier had resisted sending forces without a clear mandate, Powell's deputy announced at this meeting that if U.S. forces were needed, "We can do the job."[45] When President Bush (who recently had lost his bid for re-election) met with his senior National Security Council advisers on November 25, he chose the most forceful option—to offer U.S. troops to lead a UN action.[46] Acting Secretary of State Lawrence S. Eagleburger argued that the decision was made because of the "massive proportions" of the tragedy and because the United States "could do something" about it.[47] The U.S. mission to the United Nations also argued that Somalia provided the opportunity to increase

UN credibility in peacekeeping in the post–cold war era, a policy advocated by Bush as part of his "new world order."[48]

After reviewing UN policy options, Boutros-Ghali proposed to the Security Council on November 30 that it approve the U.S. offer.[49] After some negotiations over whether U.S. forces wouldbe under international or American command,[50] the Security Council passed Resolution 794 on December 3, approving the use of "all necessary means to establish as soon as possible a secure environment for humanitarian relief operations in Somalia."[51] The resolution clearly recognized that "UNOSOM's existing course would not in present circumstances be adequate to respond to the tragedy in Somalia" and that "it has become necessary to review the basic premises and principles of the United Nations effort in Somalia." The Security Council noted the political dimensions of the crisis and determined "to restore peace, stability and law and order with a view to facilitating the process of a political settlement under the auspices of the United Nations."[52] Immediately after the Security Council adopted Resolution 794 Bush wrote Boutros-Ghali and emphasized that the mission was "limited and specific: to create security conditions which will permit the feeding of the starving Somali people and allow the transfer of this security function to the U.N. peacekeeping force."[53]

In a speech from the Oval Office on December 4, 1992, President Bush explained his reasoning for sending U.S. troops. He emphasized the limited and humanitarian nature of the mission, stating that "we do not plan to dictate political outcomes." At the same time, however, he indirectly pointed to the inherently political nature of the operation when he stated, "Our mission is humanitarian, but we will not tolerate armed gangs ripping off their own people, condemning them to death by starvation."[54] The question of how to prevent gangs from "ripping off" vulnerable Somalis without a political solution remained unasked—and hence unanswered.

Missed Opportunities and the Challenge of Preventive Diplomacy

The first lesson that is clear from the narrative above is the need to develop strategies and plans of action to manage political transition to prevent state collapse. If a new order could have followed Siad Barre with limited violence and destruction, the potential for stability clearly would increase, and the threat of massive humanitarian crisis decrease. Several plausible opportunities for such preventive diplomacy are mentioned above. The 1988 bombing of Hargeysa, the riots and massacres in Mogadishu in 1989, and the creation of the Manifesto Group in 1990 clearly warned of impending state collapse. Individual diplomats and some states made initiatives to encourage political reconciliation during this period, but the international community did not develop a comprehensive, multilateral approach.

Once Siad Barre left Mogadishu and no single movement or coalition could make an uncontested claim to national power, the international community disengaged from the political questions and concentrated on humanitarian activities. The United Nations became involved again politically with the March 1992 cease-fire negotiations, but the focus on humanitarian initiatives without a political framework failed to end the chaos. Sahnoun's innovative diplomacy may have been the appropriate strategy in early 1992 when the cease-fire was holding. The United Nations, however, acted too late and, by mid-1992, banditry and general insecurity made it difficult for a strategy based in part on local civilian groups asserting a leadership role to succeed. A small peacekeeping operation with a dynamic and creative diplomat in charge would have had a better chance to work if it had been put in place earlier in 1992. UNOSOM I and Sahnoun, it may be argued, arrived six months too late.

In hindsight, the benefits of preventive diplomacy or small peacekeeping interventions to avert state collapse and humanitarian crisis that compel large-scale peace-enforcement interventions are clear. Policymakers, of course, do not make decisions in hindsight, and it must be noted that a proposal to send even a small peacekeeping force to Somalia before 1992 would have been regarded as a radical overreaction and a waste of scarce international resources.

4

The Political Dimensions of Peace Enforcement

The lessons of the attempts by the international community to promote political reconciliation in Somalia are ambiguous and complex. As the international operation evolved, different organizational imperatives and perspectives led to different ad hoc political strategies. The small and militarily weak UN Military Operation in Somalia (UNOSOM I) had a diplomatic strategy but lacked the capacity to pressure militia leaders. The large and powerful U.S.-led United Task Force (UNITAF) had the resources but insisted that its mandate was limited and nonpolitical. The still large but militarily and organizationally weaker UNOSOM II had more ambitious goals but lacked a viable, coherent political strategy.

The story is complicated further as different components and individuals within each phase of the international operation pursued divergent if not contradictory agendas. Differences were sharp among officials in New York, Washington, Rome, and other capitals, who produced ideas in response to their perceptions of developments, and international agents in the field, who by necessity had to react quickly to a different set of rapidly changing and confusing events on the ground.

Somali actors, at the same time, in an effort to gain or maintain power, pursued diverse strategies that changed in response to the incentives and constraints emanating from the international community. A wide range of Somali organizations and leaders sprouted in response to the resources flowing from the United Nations and international nongovernmental organizations. Quite naturally, ambitious Somali leaders resisted UN control when and where they could, cooperated when resistance seemed counterproductive, and continuously tested the limits.

Models of Action

Despite President George Bush's efforts to minimize the scope of the U.S. intervention and limit it to humanitarian purposes, the presence of a substantial international force inevitably and fundamentally altered the political landscape in Somalia.[1] Although the restrictions imposed by Washington made explicit consideration of the political implications of intervention more difficult, authorities quickly recognized that their actions had consequences for Somali politics.

The international community's political actions relating to political reconciliation in Somalia wavered between two implicit strategies developed to relate the international forces to a political framework (see appendix A). The two archetypes, labeled "Accommodate Existing Forces" and "Encourage New Institutions," start with the recognition that political reconciliation and the regeneration of institutions should be the focus of an intervention when the state has collapsed. The models diverge, however, based on the judgment made about the underlying conditions present in the state at the time of intervention. The most important variable is the character of the forces and organizations that have survived the collapse of the state: Can they serve as the building blocks for a new, sustainable order? Depending on how that question is answered, two distinctive political strategies and their operational implications emerge.

The Accommodate Existing Forces model is based on the judgment that the most powerful actors that survived state collapse have the potential to form a new, sustainable order, and the goal of the intervention therefore is to facilitate a modus vivendi among these forces. Operationally, the international intervention can follow traditional UN peacekeeping doctrine with its tenets of neutrality and the consent of local forces. That type of operation will probably minimize the extent of the intervention in time, money, and casualties.

The Encourage New Institutions model, in contrast, is appropriate when the forces that developed in the violence and anarchy of state collapse cannot act as the basis of a new sustainable order. No group or coalition exists that is capable of leading the needed transition. Alternative structures from within the local society therefore must be encouraged to step forward and fill the vacuum. Because at least some of the militias and other organizations that flourished during the chaos will probably oppose such moves, alternative leaders will be intimidated and threatened into underground or exile. The multilateral intervention, therefore, will probably need to provide a "security umbrella" that will allow the segments of civil society that are capable of constructing viable and sustainable institutions of authority the time and space needed to organize. Under these conditions, the international force may need a more "muscular" and expansive mandate than traditional peacekeeping operations.

The choice of which strategy is appropriate will depend on an evaluation of the conditions and the character of social institutions, organizations, and leaders that survived the anarchy. Clearly, the challenges for the international community are easier when its strategies can be aimed at accommodating existing forces rather than creating new institutions. The nature of the conditions and the character of the forces on the ground, however, not wishful thinking, must serve as the starting point for designing a successful political program. Unless the strategy relates to the facts on the ground there is little chance for success.

These two conceptual models are not mutually exclusive. Because each is based on different underlying conditions, and conditions will vary, the most effective strategy will change as well. In Somalia, for example, an Accommodate Existing Forces model may have been most appropriate in the initial stages of the intervention and in areas such as the northwest (Somaliland) and northeast, where local institutions maintained relative law and order. An Encourage New Institutions framework, however, may have been needed in areas such as parts of southern Somalia, where militia groups lacked local legitimacy and gained power through intimidation and looting. Over time a successful strategy might shift from accommodation to facilitating institutionalization as security increases.

Furthermore, a reliable judgment about the character of the existing forces, and hence the appropriate political strategy, will be difficult if not impossible to make *a priori*. Some groups may welcome a new security environment that allows them to put down their guns while others may not. Past behavior may indicate which groups are least likely to transform themselves into viable political players, but group goals and methods do change as the context changes. It is only by constructing a series of opportunities to test a group's intentions—giving them a real chance to prove their capacity and willingness to act as peaceful political actors—that reliable conclusions may be reached. In other words, rather than guessing or prejudging whether one or another group should be regarded as a part of a sustainable solution or as an illegitimate obstruction, a successful strategy should include a process whereby each group has the chance to behave as a legitimate political actor.

U.S. Intervention and Political Reconciliation

Following Bush's offer to provide the forces to lead an international intervention, Washington recognized that it quickly needed to establish a diplomatic and political structure capable of facilitating the major deployment authorized by UN Resolution 794. Bush named Robert Oakley, a former ambassador to Somalia and a well-respected career diplomat, as his special envoy. Oakley and his colleagues in a hastily assembled U.S. Liaison Office (USLO) began talks with militia leaders even before troops arrived.[2]

The Unified Task Force—Paving the Way for Humanitarian Operations

In December 1992, the intervention in Somalia naturally focused on the massive task of deploying thousands of troops, securing airports and other transportation facilities, moving tons of matériel in support of the troops, and distributing vast quantities of relief food to remote villages and other famine locations. This extraordinary logistical feat prevented massive starvation and clearly represented a major accomplishment of the international intervention.[3] To make this impressive operation possible, Oakley conducted a string of ad hoc meetings and reached a *modus vivendi* with various militia leaders. The U.S. armed forces organized in UNITAF took the lead in this phase of the operation. UNITAF coordinated with UNOSOM I and kept UN officials briefed, but the impetus for action came from UNITAF.

As noted, General Mohamed Farah Aideed, leader of the Somali National Alliance (SNA), and one faction of the United Somali Congress (USC), had frustrated the United Nations and had made UNOSOM I ineffective by restricting the deployment of the UN Pakistani troops to the airport. The militia leader welcomed the introduction of U.S. forces, however, in part because he recognized the futility of resisting such a powerful force and in part because he perceived that they would forestall any idea by UN Secretary General Boutros Boutros-Ghali to deploy UN troops and impose a UN "trusteeship."[4] Oakley met with Aideed and interim "president" Ali Mahdi and prodded them to sign a seven-point cease-fire and general truce agreement on December 11, 1992.[5]

Some objected that Oakley's accommodation of militia leaders in December gave them inappropriate legitimacy. One news account stated that U.S. officials "missed no opportunity to treat Aideed and Ali Mahdi with public respect," and as a result that the militia leaders "were cloaked by their American interlocutors in the mantle of legitimate power."[6] Oakley, however, made the tactical decision that the effective and safe deployment of the UNITAF force required the cooperation of the militia leaders in control of Mogadishu. Following a December 28 meeting with Oakley at the U.S. mission, Aideed and Ali Mahdi announced that they would lead a peace march across the Green Line that divided Mogadishu.[7]

Once U.S. forces had taken effective control of Mogadishu and its critical transportation facilities, Oakley expanded his negotiations into the countryside. Oakley traveled to most areas in advance of U.S. forces and negotiated with local militia and other leaders to pave the way for the troops.[8] Oakley, for example, traveled to the town of Baidoa the day before the marines arrived and, in the words of one U.S. soldier, told "the warlords that the best thing to do is not to screw with us."[9] As a result, most of the heavy weapons were moved to the countryside, and the marines met no resistance. Oakley was very successful in these talks, allowing UNITAF to move more quickly and without the use of force into the countryside. As a result, U.S. forces never reached their proposed level of 28,000 because of the ease of the initial deployment.[10]

UNITAF's area of operation was confined to the southern third of Somalia. The northwestern region, controlled by the Somali National Movement (SNM), and the northeastern region, controlled by the Somali Salvation Democratic Front (SSDF), had not fallen into the same level of violence and anarchy as the southern region. The United States and the United Nations paid scant attention to these relatively peaceful regions and did not even provide significant assistance to encourage the maintenance of stability. The ability of the SNM and the SSDF to serve as the basis for a rudimentary order in their respective regions indicates that some Somali organizations were acting effectively.

Despite such actions as mediating with militia leaders and brokering cease-fires, activities with inherently profound political implications, the United States officially claimed that it wanted to remain unengaged in the process of political rehabilitation. For example, when Oakley met with Aideed and Ali Mahdi in December 1992, he issued a statement that said, "This is not a political meeting at all. It's a get-acquainted meeting to discuss some of these security-related issues. I promise you the U.S. government is not going to get into drawing the possible political architecture for the future of Somalia."[11]

The extent to which U.S. officials went to avoid political involvement can be seen in their response to events in Kismayu, the southern port city occupied in December 1992 by the Ogadeni leader Colonel Omar Jess. Although Oakley stated that he had evidence that Jess murdered more than one hundred elders on December 9, immediately prior to the arrival of U.S. forces in Kismayu, he interpreted his mandate as too narrow to respond. "We are not an occupying power. We have no power of arrest. There is nothing in the Security Council resolution about war crimes."[12] Instead of acting to protect civilian leaders in Kismayu, Oakley publicly met with Jess on December 19 and negotiated the arrival of U.S. forces. Oakley's stated goal was to isolate Jess by encouraging traditional leaders. The symbolism of the Jess-Oakley meeting, however, undoubtedly suggested to traumatized and defenseless Somali civilian leaders that the international community accepted Jess as a legitimate leader. Potential rivals not murdered prior to December 19, not surprisingly, refrained from stepping forward to challenge Jess.[13]

The tensions between short-term tactics to limit the mission in terms of time, expense, and risk of casualties on the one hand and a broader strategy to facilitate political reconciliation on the other reached the surface publicly over the issue of disarmament. Boutros-Ghali, anxious to have the U.S. forces take on as much as possible while the force was muscular and popular, pushed for greater involvement in disarmament while Washington repeatedly and often testily refused.[14]

In the beginning, U.S. forces made extraordinary efforts to avoid disarmament, insisting that such actions lay outside their mission.[15] At one point, the marines withdrew upon finding an arms cache that included heavy weapons belonging to Osman Atto, a close ally of Aideed. Marine Colonel Fred Peck stated that the U.S. forces were trying to ensure the safe delivery of food, not "out to police all of Mogadishu."[16] Over time, however, U.S. forces became more involved, partly because of the need to create "zones of security" around the perimeter of U.S. facilities. In order to achieve the mission of humanitarian relief while deploying many thousands of U.S. troops, the operation inevitably required involvement in disarmament. At first only heavy weapons were confiscated and light arms kept inside vehicles were allowed.[17] UNITAF policies forced the militias to move their heavy weapons and technicals out of urban areas or into designated and monitored cantonments. By January 1993, however, U.S. Marines conducted large raids on the city's arms markets and even searched houses for weapons.[18]

Disarmament without a broad strategy to create a secure environment was unlikely to succeed because Somalis naturally hedged their bets and hid guns until it was clear that they could be secure without them. The hidden guns were, by themselves, little threat to vulnerable Somalis; the lack of institutionalized law and order was. Furthermore, some have suggested that ad hoc, unbalanced disarmament of the type practiced by U.S. forces in December and January may have had perverse and unintended consequences. UNITAF had more success disarming merchants and the guard forces of private relief groups than it did reducing the threat from armed bandits or more organized militia groups who hid their weapons or moved them out of town.[19] Without an underlying political strategy the policy of disarmament in Somalia reduced the ability of individuals to defend themselves without them offering an alternative means to achieve security.

The U.S. forces also became more deeply engaged in assisting the reestablishment of the police, prisons, and judiciary because the absence of such institutions risked involving U.S. forces more directly into civil administration. Initially the United States had expected to leave the task of reforming a Somali police force to the United Nations, but after marines became involved in fire-fights on the streets, Oakley decided that efforts by Somalis to reestablish the police could not wait. Without an effective Somali police force, for example, U.S. Marines became directly involved in providing security against bandits on the street, a dangerous job for which they were ill prepared. Oakley recognized "We need a police force so we can pull out."[20] The U.S. envoy held talks with Aideed and Ali Mahdi in Mogadishu on organizing a joint police force in late January.[21] Similarly, despite a reluctance to become involved in the longer-term needs of rehabilitating Somalia's destroyed economy and infrastructure, to facilitate deployment U.S. forces became increasingly engaged in clearing roads and rebuilding airports.[22]

Given the more immediate and dramatic imperative to facilitate an unprecedented movement of U.S. military forces and humanitarian aid with very little time or preparation, Oakley made the obvious and pragmatic decision that he had to make deals with any leader who had the power to prevent smooth deployment or to resist with sufficient force to cause casualties.[23] Militia leaders such as Aideed and Ali Mahdi around Mogadishu, and Omar Jess and Mohammed Siad Hersi "Morgan" around Kismayu clearly had this capacity. Avoiding armed clashes with them while managing the introduction of thousands of troops, humanitarian workers, journalists, and other officials was the overriding imperative.

Although the presence of thousands of U.S. troops and the resulting interactions with various Somali groups intrinsically involved UNITAF deeply in politics, U.S. diplomats went to extraordinary lengths to maintain their official distance from political issues. The United States, for example, did not send officials from Mogadishu to the January conference in Addis Ababa.[24] Oakley explicitly sought to avoid a political role because of the lessons he drew from Vietnam, where he served as a political officer in the 1960s.[25]

Although they were not identified as a political strategy, the ad hoc tactical decisions made by Oakley to deal with militia leaders inevitably had long-term political consequences that should have been carefully considered in advance. U.S. actions implicitly suggested an Accommodate Existing Forces strategy, at least initially. The leaders of UNITAF, however, had difficulty developing a long-term strategy for dealing with the underlying problem of political collapse because political leaders in Washington insisted that the mission remain focused on short-term humanitarian goals. If long-term political reconciliation was mentioned it was vaguely referred to as something for the United Nations to consider, not the United States. The decisions regarding the treatment of militia leaders needed to be made with reference to a coordinated, longer-term political strategy to promote reconciliation and institutional rehabilitation.

Some observers trace the origin of the difficulties the United Nations had in late 1993 to the political strategy pursued by the United States in late 1992. U.S. officials decided in December 1992 to negotiate with the militia leaders and give them reserved places in a proposed interim governing authority. In exchange, Aideed and others allowed the U.S. forces to deploy and provide humanitarian assistance unhindered. Journalist Keith Richburg characterized this arrangement as "a kind of mutual nonaggression pact that allowed U.S. troops to aid famine victims unimpeded and let Aideed keep the bulk of his weapons in depots around Mogadishu."[26] A strategy of accommodation may have been appropriate and inevitable in the early stages of the intervention. The character of the forces receiving attention and the relationship between the initial cease-fire agreements and a longer-term imperative to build sustainable institutions, however, remained unexamined.

Addis Ababa I—January 1993

On January 4, 1993, less than a month after U.S. forces landed in Mogadishu, representatives of fourteen Somali factions met in Addis Ababa under the auspices of the United Nations to begin discussions on a formula for political reconciliation (see appendix B for a list of Somali participants).[27] Secretary General Boutros Boutros-Ghali opened the talks, and the head of UNOSOM's political division, Leonard Kapungu, managed them in Special Envoy Ismat Kittani's absence. The secretary general was greeted by demonstrations, reportedly encouraged by Aideed, when he passed through Mogadishu on his way to Addis Ababa, indicating that at least some did not support his reconciliation efforts. Boutros-Ghali stated that the aim of the talks was "to make Somalis feel they are participating in their own national rehabilitation and that the thousands of soldiers and relief workers in their country are not a foreign army of occupation."[28] Besides this reassuring message, Secretary General Boutros-Ghali emphasized that the window of opportunity created by the international intervention would not remain open for long: "The world could forget Somalia in a few minutes."[29] The United Nations took the lead in organizing the Addis Ababa talks while Oakley continued his activities in support of UNITAF.[30]

Participation in the January Addis Ababa meeting was determined by the United Nations, specifically by Kapungu. Initially only twelve were invited, but the United Nations added two new factions at the last minute.[31] All the Somali invitees were clan-based organizations. Often these clan-based movements had two competing factions: one led by militia leaders who had fought to overthrow Siad Barre, the other by leaders who had aligned themselves with the Manifesto Group that tried to remove Barre by negotiations. By 1993 both factions had militias, but this difference in strategy dating back to 1989 continued to divide various clans. The United Somali Congress (USC), Somali Democratic Movement (SDM), Somali Patriotic Movement (SPM), and Somali Salvation Democratic Front (SSDF) each sent two factions to Addis Ababa.

Aideed and his allies initially resisted the Addis Ababa conference, partly because of Aideed's distrust of Boutros-Ghali and the United Nations and partly because of his demand for a special status commensurate with his role in toppling Siad Barre.[32] At the moment Aideed was obstructing the UN talks, the United States attacked one of his camps in Mogadishu with 400 marines, capturing a large quantity of weapons and reducing the camp to rubble.[33] After calculating the costs of remaining obdurate, Aideed chose to participate.

The militia leaders, after heated arguments and intense pressure from UN officials and Ethiopian President Meles Zenawi, signed an agreement that declared a cease-fire and called for a National Reconciliation Conference.[34] Essentially the Addis Ababa agreement of January 1993 assigned the contentious issues of determining the agenda of and participants in a future political conference to an ad hoc committee of militia representatives.[35] The agreement represented the continuation of the international community's strategy of catering to militia leaders and the beginnings of a strategy to foster new institutions.

Nonmilitary leaders, such as elders, intellectuals, businessmen, religious leaders, and representatives of Somali nongovernment organizations did not sign the agreements and were peripheral players for the most part.[36] As a result, the Addis Ababa meetings established the principle that, in the eyes of the United Nations at least, political rehabilitation focused on reconciling militia leaders.[37] One long-time Somali watcher concluded that "the UN's boosting of the militia leaders at the expense of the traditional leadership may turn out to be a major obstacle for peace in Somalia."[38] The human rights group Africa Watch warned that "entering into a dialogue with these thuggish leaders may well prevent attacks on American troops, but in the process unsavory and murderous characters are given a legitimacy they do not deserve."[39]

UN Special Representative Ismat Kittani stated that the progress made at the January Addis Ababa meeting meant that "we have moved from an almost impossible situation to a very difficult situation—which is a great improvement."[40] Setbacks in following up on the agreements came quickly. The first ad hoc committee meeting to discuss the agenda of the next round of talks took place on January 22 but immediately collapsed as Aideed's SNA alleged cease-fire violations by the Somali Patriotic Movement and Somali National Front around Kismayu.[41] The militias' proclaimed commitment to work toward political reconciliation lasted only a week.

While the United Nations was struggling to keep the fractious southern Somali factions engaged in talks, northern Somali leaders organized and conducted their own political reconciliation conference.[42] Following serious fighting between the Isse Muse and Habir Unis subclans in northern Somalia in 1992, which threatened to derail Somaliland's bid for independence, meetings among elders were held to help manage the conflicts. These meetings resulted in the Borama conference of elders that lasted from January through May 1993 when the conference selected a new president and vice president of Somaliland.[43] This process was endorsed by the Somali National Movement (SNM) but represented a more broadly based effort. Official representatives numbered 150, with 88 from the Isaq clan, 21 from Gadabursi, 21 Dolbahante, 11 Warsangeli, and 9 Issa. Borama town itself was in Gadabursi, not Isaq, territory. This conference gave the government of Somaliland a local legitimacy beyond the Isaq-dominated SNM.[44]

The most enduring outcome of the January Addis Ababa meetings was the establishment of the key political organizations and leaders as seen by the United Nations. The fourteen militia groups identified by the United Nations who participated in the talks and signed the Addis Ababa agreement henceforth became the major players in future efforts to spark political reconciliation. The selection of these fourteen factions, who came to be treated as something like political parties by the United Nations and other international actors, was based on a casual and haphazard process on the eve of the meetings. No thought was given as to whether these groups or individuals had the greatest potential to sustain a new order.

Aideed and factions loosely allied with him fought for a greater voice for those leaders most involved in the military campaign to overthrow Barre. According to Aideed aide Mohamed Hassan Awale: "Those who fought hardest against Siad Barre must have a greater say in the future of Somalia. You have to have a sense of fairness and justice."[45] Ali Mahdi, Aideed's rival in the United Somali Congress, and other groups who feared domination by Aideed, argued for a broader base of participation that would include community leaders, intellectuals, and representatives of women's groups.[46] Ali Mahdi ally and Somali Salvation Democratic Front leader General Mohamed Abshir Musse suggested an alternative basis of fairness and justice to determine who should participate: "The national conference should have as broad a participation as possible so that it will be more legitimate in the eyes of the people. No one group should be excluded or diminished."[47]

Rather than accept the clan militias as the inevitable basis of social and political reconciliation, an alternative perspective would suggest that the real division in Somalia was the armed and powerful versus the unarmed and vulnerable. One Somali NGO leader stated, "Its the tough and the vicious versus the peaceful and the weak."[48] Given the brutality of 1991 and 1992, legitimate leaders and spokespersons were reluctant to step forward until they had strong evidence that the militia leaders and bandits would not target them for so doing. Former Somali police chief Ahmed Jama Mousa observed, "People are still afraid to raise their voices because of the danger of being knocked off."[49] The question, as Kittani later put it, is not who will speak for the Somalis but rather, "Which Somalis are able to speak freely?"[50]

"Plucking the Bird" in February

Despite the dominance of militia chiefs at the January 1993 Addis Ababa talks, UNITAF sent clear messages to the armed factions that force would be used against them if they violated certain rules. U.S. Cobra gunships attacked gunmen loyal to militia-leader Morgan as he moved toward the southern port city of Kismayu in late January, destroying several of his armed vehicles. According to Oakley, the purpose of the attack was to "teach General Morgan a lesson."[51] Despite this action, Morgan managed to infiltrate his supporters into Kismayu where they engaged the forces of Aideed ally Omar Jess. In late February, Oakley sent an ultimatum to Morgan, ordering him to leave Kismayu and encamp his forces: "If any of your forces are found outside of these locations on Feb. 26 or thereafter, they will be engaged."[52]

U.S. officials believed that UNITAF actions, by seizing some weapons, encouraging factional leaders to move many of their heavy guns and technicals to remote areas, limiting looting, and forcing at least some militia elements into camps, inherently reduced the power of the gunmen. In a March 1993 report Boutros-Ghali stated clearly that "UNITAF's presence in key areas of the country has reduced the influence of those whose power was based on their heavy weapons."[53]

The counterpart to limiting the militia leaders' power was encouraging alternative, nonmilitia leaders. Oakley used his personal prestige to engage leaders from Somali civil society. Various groups used the U.S. Liaison Office as a neutral meeting place, and Oakley served as a facilitator of discussions about Somalia's future. Oakley recognized that such meetings encouraged alternative leaders to find their voice and thereby helped shift power away from the militias. Abdirahman Osman Raghe, a former civil servant who led one group of intellectuals stated: "For the past two years, most of the social forces—like women, intellectuals, wise men—they were silenced by the gun. With the arrival of the [UN] forces, the social forces can now talk. They can reorganize themselves."[54]

Oakley deliberately and consciously sought to tilt the balance away from the militia leaders and toward alternative, civilian groups. He referred to this strategy as "plucking the bird." According to Oakley, if "you take one feather at a time . . . the bird doesn't think there's anything terrible going on. Then one day he finds he can't fly."[55] This comment, broadcast to Somalia by the BBC, incensed many Somali militia leaders who regarded it as arrogant, thereby making it more difficult for Oakley to mediate.[56]

Oakley's efforts to reduce the power of the militia leaders had the most striking effect on Aideed, who seemed to be under pressure from a variety of fronts in late February. UNITAF's actions to disarm forces loyal to Aideed ally Omar Jess in Kismayu had the effect (if not the intention) of allowing Morgan to take control of the city. On February 24–25, 1993, riots broke out in Mogadishu, and demonstrators reportedly loyal to Aideed sacked the Egyptian embassy and attacked peacekeeping troops, wounding several Americans and Nigerians.[57] In early March, guards from Aideed's Habir Gedir clan who had worked for the United Nations and international non-governmental organizations before the intervention demanded payment for continuing to "protect" humanitarian relief operations. Aideed pressed his supporters' claims with the United Nations, but some U.S. officials, such as Walter Clarke, regarded this request as naked extortion and refused to pay.[58]

In the midst of these tensions, the United Nations called a second Addis Ababa meeting of the fourteen Somali militia leaders for March 1993. As the Somalis prepared to travel to Addis Ababa for the talks and assessed their futures, they had mixed signals from the international community. On the one hand, the United Nations clearly considered the militia leaders the major political players in a peace settlement, meeting and consulting with them often and making them the focus of the Addis Ababa meetings. On the other hand, actions against Morgan around Kismayu and against Aideed in Mogadishu suggested that the international force would limit the militia leaders' maneuvering room. Nonmilitia figures who were trying to determine whether they could step forward and assert their authority against the gunmen might be encouraged by some of the assertive enforcement actions of UNITAF, but they would also be concerned about the dominant role of military figures in the Addis Ababa meetings. The international community seemed to be pursuing two different strategies, one to accommodate the militia leaders and the other to encourage rival leaders from civil society.

Addis Ababa II—March 1993

The basis for the March meetings in Addis Ababa had been worked out by the ad hoc committee established by the militias in consultation with the United Nations after the first Addis Ababa.[59] The United Nations eventually obtained enough of a consensus to issue invitations to the same groups that participated in the January talks and additional "political movements, community, religious and women's groups, civic and non-governmental organizations (NGOs) as well as elders and eminent persons."[60] UN officials claimed that the March meeting "will be among a wide group of Somalis, from all sectors of society, and could thereby contribute to broad-based and lasting solutions."[61]

Immediately before the political meeting, the United Nations held a donors' conference, chaired by Under Secretary General for Humanitarian Affairs Jan Eliasson, to devise a program for humanitarian assistance. This event had the intended effect of bringing in a number of officials from Somali nongovernmental organizations to Addis Ababa to be present when the militia leaders arrived. Indeed, the March meeting brought together the widest range of Somali leaders since the ouster of Siad Barre.[62] At one point, Somali women in attendance began a hunger strike to increase pressure on the factions to reach agreement.[63] Some 250 Somalis participated in one way or another, but in the end it was the fourteen militia leaders with whom the United Nations negotiated the agreement.[64] Some observers objected that the United Nations "treated [the warlords] as honored dignitaries [and] . . . caved into one power play after another."[65] A UN official reportedly stated, "I have never in my 12 years with the U.N. seen it give in to men like this. . . . These are common criminals. It is shameful."[66]

The March deliberations were characterized by a rift between two groupings of Somali militia leaders. Conference participants differed on whether the reconciliation plan should move toward reconstruction of local administrative structures on a decentralized, regional basis or should start with a national framework.[67] Aideed and his allies favored the regional framework because it gave greater power to clan-based militias while a group around Ali Mahdi favored a stronger national government to protect clans with weaker military forces.[68]

The conference began on March 15 and lasted for three and a half weeks. Immediately before the meeting, the political leadership of the international operation changed. Oakley returned to Washington, and Robert Gosende, a U.S. Information Agency official who previously had served in Somalia, replaced him as U.S. special envoy. Special Representative of the Secretary General Ismat Kittani, whose ill health limited his activity, was replaced by U.S. Admiral (Ret.) Jonathan Howe. Newly arrived UN Deputy Special Representative Lansana Kouyate, a respected and energetic young Guinean diplomat, and Meles Zenawi, the transitional president of Ethiopia, managed the talks and kept the diplomatic pressure on the Somali factional chiefs.

The Addis Ababa conference broke up temporarily when Aideed's SNA walked out in protest over resumed fighting in Kismayu between SNA's ally Jess and SNF forces under Morgan.[69] Although some details are murky, several hundred Morgan fighters apparently attacked a much smaller group of troops loyal to Jess, forcing them to flee the city on March 16. The United States had forced Morgan to withdraw from Kismayu in late February and then turned the city over to Belgian forces.[70] The attack apparently took the Belgian peacekeepers in Kismayu by surprise: once Morgan had infiltrated the city the Belgians had the unenviable choice of opening fire on civilian crowds or simply watching the battle take place.[71] U.S. quick-reaction forces prevented a Jess counterattack, thereby creating the impression to some that the United States and the United Nations supported Morgan's position.[72] The Addis Ababa talks broke down in chaos as Aideed accused Morgan of intentionally disrupting the talks; Ali Mahdi accused Jess of the same. The United Nations sent a delegation representing all fourteen factions to Kismayu to investigate.

After lengthy but inconclusive talks and several near breakdowns, UN negotiators Kouyate and Ethiopian President Meles produced a compromise agreement and presented it to the fourteen factions on March 27. The final meetings took place in the Royal Palace in Addis Ababa with just Kouyate and Meles present with the factional leaders. Kouyate and Meles made it clear that if the factions refused to settle their differences and accept a compromise without further delay, the United Nations would close the conference and look elsewhere for Somali leadership or disengage from the conflict.[73]

The Addis Ababa agreement called for a Transitional National Council (TNC) to act as the prime political authority for a two-year transitional period. The council would have seventy-four seats. Each of the fifteen factions would have one seat, and each of the eighteen regions would send three representatives, one of whom must be a woman. Mogadishu would be represented by Ali Mahdi and four others. A rotating president would serve as the national executive. Central administrative departments, staffed by professionals and under the oversight of the TNC, would be responsible for reinstating government services. District councils, composed of locally selected representatives, would be created in each district and send representatives to regional councils. These eighteen regional councils would operate with a high level of autonomy. The relationship between regional and central administration remained vague. The agreement called for "complete, impartial, and transparent" disarmament within ninety days. It also provided for the appointment of a Transitional Charter Drafting Committee and a committee chaired by Aideed to resolve outstanding issues with the Somali National Movement.[74]

The agreement represented a compromise between the factions allied with Aideed's Somali National Alliance (SNA) and twelve rival factions loosely allied with Ali Mahdi. The SNA wanted the TNC to be composed of representatives nominated by the political factions to serve as Somalia's supreme political and administrative authority. The group of twelve wanted a weak, "symbolic" TNC composed of clan representatives. Aideed and his allies hoped to keep government in the hands of regionally based clan organizations.[75]

The Addis Ababa agreement did not presume to settle all issues and, given the time constraints and polarized positions of the major actors, represented a potentially important first step. The agreement remained silent on several troublesome matters and lacked effective implementation or enforcement mechanisms. For example, the agreement said nothing about how the membership of the TNC would be determined. District councils would send representatives to regional councils, but the Addis Ababa agreement stated merely that district council members "shall be appointed through election or through consensus-based selection in accordance with Somali traditions."[76] Furthermore, rapid and simultaneous disarmament and encampment of militias was pledged, but no mechanism was established to ensure what was inherently a contentious task. The agreement enumerated the components of an agreement without specifying how to arrive at it.[77] Still, as Oakley put it, the agreement was "an important step forward but it's not the end of the process."[78]

The Addis Ababa agreement spoke about "Somalia as a whole" and, the eighteen regions referred to in the framework included five within the northeastern region controlled by the Somali National Movement (SNM). The

Isaq-based SNM, however, did not sign the agreement and insisted that the region was the independent Somaliland Republic. Mohammed Ibrahim Egal, the prime minister of Somalia immediately before Barre's coup in 1969 and the president of Somaliland after the Borama meetings of 1993, addressed the conference but only to bring a message of peace. He reiterated the SNM's determination to await reconciliation in the south before any talks with Somaliland officials could take place. Three movements representing smaller clans in the north who opposed the Isaq-dominated SNM's rule, participated in the Addis Ababa meetings and signed the document, making SNM officials more suspicious about the process. As one European observer phrased it, from Somaliland's point of view, the Addis Ababa formula "intends the northern independent republic to be ruled by the muddled setup of committees presided over by the southern former warlords (they are now called politicians)."[79]

Despite these and other flaws, the Addis Ababa agreements of March 1993 represented the clearest and most fully articulated strategy for promoting political rehabilitation in Somalia since the state collapsed. Although the agreements were vague on certain critical details and were negotiated among a small group of militia leaders, the settlement offered a broad, preliminary framework for reconciliation. The agreement had elements of a strategy to accommodate the existing forces by focusing political power among the fourteen factions identified in the January Addis Ababa meeting. At the same time, by including regional and district assemblies, the agreements provided a mechanism for nonmilitia participation. If successfully implemented, the design could make the transition from a political strategy of short-term accommodation to a longer-term strategy of building new institutions. The framework gave the militia leaders the opportunity to demonstrate their commitment to reconciliation and broad-based power sharing, to make the transition from warlords to statesmen. The international community had a chance to demonstrate its interest in political reconstruction by putting resources behind implementing the agreement and keeping the diplomatic pressure on the factions to honor their commitments. If the Addis Ababa agreements had been implemented, prospects for a new, sustainable order would have been greatly increased.

Failure to Implement Addis Ababa—March–June 1993[80]

In the midst of the negotiations in Addis Ababa and the important period of implementation in late March 1993, the international operation simultaneously went through an organizational and leadership transition. UNITAF, the operation under the military command of U.S. Marine Lieutenant General Robert B. Johnson and the diplomatic leadership of U.S. Envoy Robert Oakley, began to wind down. UNOSOM II, a more internationalized force commanded by Turkish Lieutenant General Cevik Bir and led politically by UN Special Representative Jonathan Howe, moved into its place.[81] Although the formal date of transfer of command was May 4, Oakley left to be replaced by Robert Gosende at the U.S. Liaison Office and Kittani's position as UN special representative was filled by Jonathan Howe in early March.

The transition was made more difficult because the United Nations and Secretary General Boutros-Ghali intentionally dragged their feet in a bid to force the United States to shoulder more of the burden. The United Nations hoped to push the United States into more involvement in disarmament before turning responsibility over to a less well-armed operation. What officials initially had hoped would be a "seamless transition" was to become an "unseemly" one.[82] Partly as a result of that development, UNOSOM II began its mission seriously understaffed and without the necessary forces to assume the responsibilities held by U.S. troops. Howe's first weeks therefore were consumed with his efforts to construct the type of organization he thought necessary for the task rather than with focusing on implementing the Addis Ababa agreements.

The UN Security Council adopted Resolution 814 on March 26, the day before the militia leaders accepted the Addis Ababa agreements. This resolution expanded the mandate of UN troops, including enforcement actions under Chapter VII of the UN Charter, to establish a secure environment. This new mandate explicitly included disarmament, the establishment of a police force, and national reconciliation. The resolution authorized actions "to assist the people of Somalia to promote and advance political reconciliation through broad participation by all sectors of Somali society, and the re-establishment of national and regional institutions and civil administration in the entire country."[83] This resolution seemed to be consistent with the March framework developed in Addis Ababa. In fact, the Secretary General released a press statement that welcomed the Addis Ababa agreement as "an important achievement of the Somali people, the first positive step following the adoption . . . of Resolution 814."[84]

The Addis Ababa agreement called on the United Nations and UNOSOM "to extend all necessary assistance to the people of Somalia for the implementation of this agreement."[85] Time was short because the TNC was supposed to be established in forty-five days. Kouyate and his staff developed a list of possible ways in which UNOSOM could help in implementing the agreement, such as providing consultants to assist the Charter Drafting Committee, offering support services (logistics, financial) for committee meetings, and engaging observers to assist in selection processes for district and regional councils.[86]

During April Mogadishu was as peaceful as it had been since Siad Barre's downfall. The promises of peace contained in the Addis Ababa agreement were sufficient to raise the hopes of many residents that the cycle of violence soon would end. Militia leaders gave interviews and tried to convince Western journalists that they had always favored democracy and wanted to be called "freedom fighters" rather than "warlords."[87]

More important in Kouyate's view than any specific outcome of Addis Ababa meetings was the adoption of the principle that negotiations must be the means of reaching agreement. Kouyate believed that the Addis Ababa agreement, although signed only by militia leaders, could be the starting point for a bottom-up strategy that would diminish the dominant role of the armed groups. The selection of district and regional councils would provide the opening that would enable the broader Somali civil society to be included in the process. Kouyate proposed forming selection committees to determine the respective district councils. Members of the committees would be prohibited from serving on the councils.[88] Although not mentioned specifically in the Addis Ababa agreements, UNOSOM hoped that the selection committees would broaden participation. Kouyate pledged that the fourteen militias who signed the agreement would not be allowed to "hijack" or dominate the process of selection.[89] Regardless of its numerous specific weaknesses, Kouyate argued that the Addis Ababa agreement was a Somali-generated first step that deserved follow-up by international actors.[90]

Despite Kouyate's crucial role in the Addis Ababa talks, the new UN team in Mogadishu led by Howe was skeptical. Howe, the head of UNOSOM's political division Leonard Kapungu, and others believed that the agreement enshrined the militia leaders as the dominant, legitimate leaders of Somalia. Howe saw little reason to expect the factional leaders to live up to the agreement, and he refused to meet with the signatories. Kouyate and others argued that the factional leaders should not be ignored but rather encouraged through the agreement to make the switch from warlord to statesmen.[91]

Ambassador Robert Gosende, the new head of the U.S. Liaison Office (USLO), also was critical of the agreement.[92] Gosende argued that UNOSOM should focus on achieving a cease-fire and on reconstructing and rehabilitating civil society, not on reconciling militia leaders. According to Kouyate, "Gosende fears that the warlords will dominate and manipulate the political process at the expense of the Somali people."[93] In the U.S. official's view, the underlying security problem required institutions (including Somali police and judiciary) capable of challenging the militia leaders, not an agreement that strengthened and institutionalized the gunmen.[94] All parties agreed that an institutionalized Somali order was needed, but they differed on the roles the militia leaders originally accommodated by the international community should play.

UNOSOM did act to set up the district and regional councils, working first in the areas with the greatest stability and postponing action in contested areas like Kismayu, Gagadud, and Baidoa. In Bossaso, for example, a regional town in the northeast where the Somali Salvation Democratic Front maintained relative peace, UNOSOM consulted with SSDF leader Abshir Musse and elders and quickly reached an agreement to appoint a twenty-one-member district council.[95] By October 1993, thirty-eight of the proposed sixty-one district councils had been formed along with two regional councils.[96] Some council members, however, complained that UNOSOM provided little support to make the local administrations viable. Others complained that the councils had been formed too hastily and haphazardly, often relying on the nominees of militia chiefs, and as a result, were not truly representative.[97]

Aideed's Somali National Alliance faction accused UNOSOM of meddling in the internal affairs of the Somali people and rejected the district and regional councils altogether.[98] Some Somali groups such as the SSDF seemed prepared to institutionalize their power and make the transition from militias to regional political organizations and to operate through regional assemblies as envisioned in the Addis Ababa agreements. Other, however, such as the Somali National Alliance (SNA), indicated that unless they could control the assemblies they would use their military force to interfere with implementation.

The process of creating district assemblies therefore clearly indicated which groups were prepared to work politically. Tensions in the towns of Kismayu and Galcayo preoccupied the United Nations, further distracting it from developing a coherent strategy to follow up the Addis Ababa agreements. Morgan occupied Kismayu in March and the United Nations warned SNA member Jess to keep his distance. To Aideed and the SNA, this status was intolerable. Jess decided to ignore the warnings from the Belgian peacekeepers and attacked Kismayu. The Belgians responded with force and repulsed the SNA attack. As a result, the United Nations appeared in SNA eyes to be defending and supporting Morgan, their rival.

Another hot spot between the SNA and its rivals was the Galcayo region. This transitional region, which contains significant Mijerteen and Hawiye groups and includes Aideed's hometown, was largely under the control of General Mohamed Abshir Musse of the Mijerteen clan-based Somali Salvation Democratic Front in spring 1993, one of the factions opposed to the SNA. UN forces did not deploy in the region because the SSDF maintained security and managed relief on its own. Many of the heavy weapons and technicals removed from Mogadishu were redeployed to this area outside of UN supervision.

In mid-May, immediately after the formal transition to UNOSOM II, Aideed and one part of the SSDF led by Yusuf Abdullahi agreed to hold talks to discuss their differences, and they requested UN support. UNOSOM II officials accepted but disagreed with Aideed about the rules of the conference and who would chair. In the end, there were two conferences, one under Aideed's chairmanship and the other under UNOSOM.[99] Given this flap, neither conference managed to make progress on security in the Galcayo area.[100] According to Walter Clarke, "Some observers believe the whole Galcayo conference exercise represented an effort by Aideed to humiliate the UN and to mobilize potential allies for a military confrontation with UN forces."[101] In any event, Aideed's conference ended on June 4, the day before an attack on Pakistani peacekeepers that proved to be a political watershed.

The period between March and June 1993 may have represented the best chance for the international intervention to put in place and act on a strategy to promote political reconciliation and the reestablishment of government institutions. The agreements reached by the Somali factional leaders in Addis Ababa left several important issues unsettled. Regardless, they represented the most complete blueprint for political action put forward under UN auspices and could have served as an initial step in what would undoubtedly have been a long process of political rehabilitation.

The United Nations and United States, however, missed the opportunity to test the potential of the Addis Ababa model. The change in leadership while the talks took place meant that UN Special Representative Howe and

U.S. Special Envoy Gosende were not deeply involved in negotiating the agreements. The international officials placed a greater emphasis on clashes in Kismayu and Galcayo and on working outside the framework of the militia agreements to reconstruct Somali institutions. Furthermore, the intricate transition to UNOSOM II preoccupied the leaders with organizational questions.

Even if the international community had committed support and resources to the March Addis Ababa agreements, it is unclear whether they could have succeeded. To the extent that the United States and the United Nations had a strategy to promote political reconciliation, it straddled the critical question of which Somali groups had the potential to act as the basis for a new, sustainable political order. The Addis Ababa agreements included aspects of two fundamentally different and perhaps antithetical strategies of political reconciliation. On the one hand, the Addis Ababa meetings enshrined the militia leaders—the signatories of the agreements—as the leading players. On the other, the structure of the TNC suggested that somehow nonmilitia leaders would participate through district and regional councils.

The June 1993 Attack on Pakistani Forces

The peaceful interlude that followed the March Addis Ababa meetings did not last. By mid-May tensions rose as implementation of the agreements stalled, militia leaders began to move unilaterally to increase their power and maneuver for position, and clashes erupted around Kismayu. Observers speculated about when one or another faction would test the resolve of the new leaders of UNOSOM II. On June 5, an armed group of Somalis ambushed Pakistani UN troops and set off a politically disastrous military reaction.[102] Some of the Pakistanis were conducting a previously announced inspection of a UN-sanctioned SNA arms depot that shared a compound with General Aideed's radio station; others were killed simultaneously at a feeding center on the other side of Mogadishu, suggesting that the ambush was preplanned and coordinated.[103] Although the timing and scale of the assault surprised officials of the United States and the United Nations, the U.S. Liaison Office had issued a warning in mid-May that gunmen, reportedly aligned with Aideed, had threatened to murder Americans.[104]

The Security Council strongly condemned the "unprovoked armed attacks" and adopted Resolution 837 that authorized "all necessary measures against all those responsible" the next day. The resolution stated that the attacks had been "launched by forces apparently belonging to the United Somali Congress (USC/SNA)" led by Aideed.[105] Tom Farer, an American University professor of law and international relations with experience in Somalia, later concluded in a report to the United Nations that "clear and convincing evidence" showed that Aideed was responsible for the attacks.[106] Howe shocked the U.S. and UN military commanders in Mogadishu by placing a public price on Aideed's head, and U.S. Ambassador to the United Nations Madeleine K. Albright branded Aideed a "thug."[107] Aideed, who once had been courted by the United States and United Nations and treated as a major player in internationally sanctioned conferences on political reconciliation, was now demonized and made a pariah.

The weak, incomplete, and inconsistent U.S.-UN political strategy to encourage political reconciliation became irrelevant in the aftermath of the attack on the Pakistanis. UNOSOM and, in particular, the autonomous and U.S.-commanded Quick Reaction Force began a campaign to capture Aideed. U.S. forces bombed and strafed sections of Mogadishu and alienated much of the population. This lashing out without a political framework to guide and limit the use of force disconnected UNOSOM from any strategy of political reconciliation. Outside of the battleground of Mogadishu UN political operatives continued to encourage regional reconciliation efforts and establish district councils, but the focus of the international effort was on the search for Aideed.[108]

U.S. Casualties and Withdrawal

The United States supported the efforts by UN Special Representative Howe to capture Aideed and provided most of the forces used in the manhunt. In a brutal operation in July, U.S. helicopters destroyed a building identified as one of Aideed's headquarters, killing dozens of Somalis.[109] As U.S. casualties mounted over the summer, dissent in Washington against the Clinton administration's policies grew. Democratic Senator Robert C. Byrd called for the remaining U.S. forces to "pack up and go home" in July.[110] In August, Howe asked for additional U.S. forces, particularly the elite special operations Delta Force, to increase his ability to track Aideed through Mogadishu.[111] Secretary of Defense Les Aspin defended the administration's policy in a speech on August 27. Aspin, determined to "stay the course," stated, "We went there to save a people, and we succeeded. We are staying there now to help those same people rebuild their nation."[112] By September, Washington tried to move the focus of attention away from capturing Aideed and put in place a diplomatic strategy.[113] Gosende recognized the futility of the Aideed manhunt and sent an urgent cable that called for a shift in U.S. policy on September 17.[114]

While this debate proceeded, the U.S. commander in Mogadishu received a tip that top Aideed lieutenants would be at the Olympic Hotel. On October 3, U.S. Army Rangers conducted a daylight helicopter raid. The U.S. forces were surrounded and in the ensuing fire-fight suffered terrible casualties— 18 dead, 84 wounded, and 1 helicopter pilot captured. One Malaysian peacekeeper also was killed and seven were wounded. Somali leaders estimated their casualties at 312 killed and 814 wounded.[115]

Within hours, horrifying pictures appeared on U.S. television networks: the corpses of American soldiers being dragged through the streets of Mogadishu, a bloodied and terrified helicopter pilot being held hostage. These pictures generated a powerful, visceral reaction among Americans. The public had been given no explanation for why troops were in Somalia other than to feed the hungry, and so the reaction was strong. After having been promised cost-free international order, the public resented the price being paid. As the *New York Times* put it, "Americans were told that their soldiers were being sent to work in a soup kitchen and they were understandably shocked to find them in house-to-house combat."[116]

Bipartisan panic swept Capitol Hill, and a poorly received briefing by Secretary of Defense Les Aspin and Secretary of State Warren Christopher on October 5 only increased anxiety.[117] To stem the growing momentum for immediate withdrawal, President Clinton made a televised Oval Office speech in which he announced he was sending more troops in the short run but promised complete withdrawal by March 31, 1994.[118] He warned that "our own credibility with friends and allies would be severely damaged" if the United States "cut and ran" before then.[119] In the end, Washington took the advice that it had long rejected once before in Vietnam: declare victory and get out.

Final Attempts at Political Reconciliation

Clinton sent Ambassador Oakley back to Mogadishu in an attempt to create sufficient order for U.S. withdrawal without additional political damage in the aftermath of the October debacle. The Somali factions met again at UN-sponsored talks in Addis Ababa in November–December 1993. Aideed boycotted the talks until December 2 when the United States transported him directly to Addis Ababa in a military aircraft. Nonmilitia leaders, viewing the dominating role of militia leaders and the rehabilitation of Aideed, retreated from the challenge of political reconciliation. Ethiopian leader Meles Zenawi tried again to pressure the Somalis to accept an agreement but ended up storming out of the meeting and saying, "It appears you Somalis are not willing to reconcile. Goodbye."[120] No agreement was reached.

Despite the failure of political reconciliation talks, the United States and most European states withdrew their forces in early 1994. These troops were replaced to an extent by forces from India, Pakistan, Egypt, and Malaysia. In May 1994, another round of UN-sponsored talks took place in Nairobi. Lansana Kouyate, the special representative following Howe, again managed to get the major militia leaders to sign paper commitments to begin political reconciliation but, as was the case with the earlier UN-brokered agreements, fighting broke out almost instantly.

By mid-1994 UNOSOM had largely abandoned any pretense of political or security objectives. The foreign troops rarely left their bases, gunmen and technicals returned to the streets, and looting, kidnappings for ransom, and general insecurity led many international nongovernmental organizations to withdraw again. As one journalist characterized the sense of despair: "In the 18 months since the first UN troops were sent to Somalia to protect humanitarian supplies at the height of the country's war-induced famine, UNOSOM has failed either to disarm the factions or provide an alternative to the gun. Doomed to be the impotent spectators of renewed factional fighting in Mogadishu, UN troops now face increasing difficulty in keeping even themselves alive."[121] Keith B. Richburg summed up the United Nations' accomplishments: "After the deaths of more than 100 U.N. peacekeepers here—including 36 Americans—Somalia is as unstable and devoid of hope today as at any time since it collapsed into anarchy in January 1991."[122] Some diplomats and observers suggested that perhaps Somalis would have more success reaching political reconciliation without foreign involvement.[123] In any event, the international community was disengaging, leaving Somalis to their own fate.

The Political Dimensions of Peace Enforcement

The intervention carried out by the United States and the United Nations in Somalia had many facets. The unprecedented and largely successful humanitarian operation that prevented perhaps hundreds of thousands of Somalis from dying and the tragic military campaign that failed to capture

Aideed have received deserved attention. The political dimensions of the intervention—often implicit and sometimes even denied—generally have been obscured by these other issues. From the beginning, however, the activities of the international community in Somalia have had significant and unavoidable implications for political reconciliation. Ambassador Robert Oakley's negotiations and agreements with militia leaders had the clear (if unintended) result of strengthening these groups relative to other potential political forces. As an initial step to facilitate deployment such cease-fire agreements are needed, but they should be considered in the context of a longer-term effort to encourage new political institutions. The very presence of international forces and the resulting reduction of looting and banditry, however, weakened the militias and encouraged Somali civilian leaders, elders, and intellectuals to begin political activities. The January 1993 talks sponsored by the United Nations in Addis Ababa had a more explicitly political strategy of creating the framework for political reconciliation by focusing on the militias. In February, the United States and United Nations gave mixed signals, encouraging nonmilitia groups and using force against the gunmen while continuing to engage the militias in talks. The next round of talks in Addis Ababa placed the factional leaders in the center of the search for a new political order but also envisioned locally selected assemblies and the participation of women.

Some have sought to explain this ambiguous record as a two-track strategy to promote political reconciliation in Somalia.[124] Each of these two tracks, however, represented a fundamentally different strategy. Rather than reinforcing or complementing each other as a carrot-and-stick diplomatic strategy might, they undercut one another: pursuing both meant neither was likely to succeed. On the one hand the highest level of officials met regularly with militia leaders, treated them as legitimate political actors, and requested their consent on operational matters. On the other hand and simultaneously, U.S. and UN officials encouraged potential alternatives and rivals to militia leaders, such as traditional elders, leaders of Somali nongovernmental organizations, women, and professionals, to assert their political role. Some militia leaders saw the threat represented by the establishment of village councils outside their control and took actions to prevent their success. Alternative civilian leaders saw the close working relationship between the militias and the international forces, felt intimidated, and consequently were reluctant to play a leadership role. In the end, therefore, neither a coalition of militia leaders nor institutions based on civilian leaders were possible. The international strategy fell between two options, accomplishing neither.

The UNITAF and UNOSOM political strategy was internally contradictory because decisionmakers never settled what attitude to take toward the militia leaders. Should the gunmen have been treated as if they were capable of acting like political parties, or should the international community have looked elsewhere for political leadership? One study group summed up this dilemma: "Those who intervene in places like Somalia must decide in advance whether they are going to accept and work with the local powers that be, even though these people may be the ones responsible for the trouble that triggered intervention. This decision is key."[125] The March 1993 Addis Ababa agreements could have helped the international community judge which leaders were interested and capable of acting as political players and which had to be prevented from acting as spoilers, destroying the effort to create a new order. Walter Clarke, who served in the U.S. Liaison Office mission in 1993, argues that "so long as the international authorities (UNOSOM I and UNITAF) deferred to the warlords and their followers— or appeared to do so—there was little likelihood that effective political processes would be established by Somalis not associated with them [the "warlords"]."[126] The international intervention, in part because it could not or would not face up to the underlying political challenges of political reconciliation in Somalia, ended the operation without introducing a new, sustainable order. The international community paid a high price but failed to leave behind the foundations upon which the Somalis could govern themselves.

5

Conclusion

The past decade has been especially painful for the Somali people and for the varied international actors who have attempted to deal with Somalia. The decomposition of the state under the authoritarian regime of Siad Barre, its complete collapse in the aftermath of his overthrow, the ensuing catastrophe manifested in social breakdown, violence, displacement, and famine, and the consequent international intervention that ended in withdrawal without a sustainable order, reflect the terrible forces that have come to occupy this tragic land. This complex and profound crisis called for creative responses by actors at all levels, from local to international. Given the depth of the degeneration of Somali political life in the 1990s, what policies and actions plausibly could have encouraged a restoration of legitimate order?

What Somalis Must Do

The collapse of the Somali state has been profound on many levels, not least of all in the destruction of a common set of normative principles or political culture necessary for group interaction and communication. The old Somali social order based on kinship, *heer*, and Islam failed to survive the pressures of new economic relations tied to production for commodity markets and new political relations arising from the creation of a centralized colonial and then independent state.

The arrival of a commodity-ordered social system that emphasized individualism and private welfare, coupled with a shrinking resource base, eroded the old linkages between blood ties and the *heer*, as well as Islamic precepts. As individuals struggled to secure a foothold in a precarious new world, *heer* was shed like an old skin or else was mutilated in a desperate attempt to fit it into new and chaotic circumstances.

The collapse of the state in the early 1990s further alienated old cultural constraints from the violent environment of everyday life. The old system of beliefs and codes of behavior suited another universe, not the strange and frightening world of living in the rubble of modern state collapse. Confronted with the loss of meaning and unable to imagine an alternative framework of rights, obligations, and responsibilities, disconnected blood-ties assumed an unprecedented place in the history of Somali peoples: they became the main prism to interpret the world they had to confront. Deprived of its civilizing aspects, raw propinquity supplanted kinship with clanism. This decoupling of blood-ties and pan-Somali lore (heer) tore traditional foundations asunder. This moral collapse in turn produced a growing number of antisocial, alienated individuals. As a result contemporary Somali society is caught in the grip of ruinous clanism unmitigated by kinship and mutual obligation, which gets more bizarre and destructive as the underlying society fails to produce a new and sustainable cultural foundation.

In Somalia, therefore, the old cultural structures have been undermined, distorted beyond their capacity to guide or constrain behavior. A new order, however, is powerless to stand up.[1] Note the cry of an eminent Somali *hobell* (troubadour). He laments,

Oh money! Oh money!
You who separates no man from real man
You are the fire that excites women
You are strength for the weak
You bring down the high and mighty
You who never lets me sleep
You are sorrow and pain
You are the lethal tongue in any debate
You are one that none can do without
You are a perpetual blessing
You are constant hassle and bother
You are the weapon that kills
You are the loot killed for
You are dignity itself
Oh money! You never let me sleep.[2]

The alienation of individuals seeking to find meaning and cultural guide-posts in circumstances where traditional culture and values no longer relate to their environment is not unique to contemporary Somalia. As Aiden Southall observes,

> Africans truly lost faith in their own cultures at a very profound level, while still clinging on to them as straws with substitutes and yearning for the values which had given meaning to life. From this arise personal dilemmas and social conflicts which on a national scale remain for the moment insoluble. Hence appear inappropriate and conflicting values and goals, loss of loyalties and solidarities, consequent abuse of power, corruption and waste of resources, none of it conducive to well-motivated and productive work, even apart from the burden of exploitation from without.[3]

Culture, however, has the capacity and power to reinvigorate itself. Both *heer* and Islam, the twin pillars of the Somali tradition, include retrievable values and an ethos that enshrine individual dignity, justice and generosity, collective struggle, and intergenerational obligations. Additionally, modernism offers new capacities (for example, reason, rationality, efficiency) that are not necessarily antithetical to the traditional mode of livelihood. A worthwhile effort toward reclamation as well as synthesis requires a new discourse of politics.

Who in Somalia can start the process of determining these structures and patterns of interaction? Answers to this question are critical not only to Somalis but to external actors anxious to promote a new order that can prevent future humanitarian crises. There is no single individual or association that is capable to undertake this task. Five constituents that together may serve as a core group to address this question may be proposed and analyzed as a preliminary response.

The first group is the elders. As is well known, each major kin family, as shown in figure 2-1, has its own elder. These traditional leaders, recognized for their knowledge of human affairs in general and in the practice of *heer* in particular, are most suitable to revive and speak for this part of Somali culture and the authority that resides within it. After being subjected to the indignities and cruelties of clanistic politics and internecine conflict, most legitimate elders continue to decry the fraudulence and violence that has engulfed Somalia.

The second category is the *Ulema* or *Sheikhs*. The burden of the theologians would be to devise ways to bring the axioms of Islam to the task of controlling and disciplining the irresponsible elements of society. The return of Islamic guidelines need not be solely construed as, in the erroneous language of the Western media, "fundamentalist."[4]

The third constituency is the modernizers—the bearers of secular ideas and practice. This group will include intellectuals, professionals, some merchants, and technocrats. A new group of organizers and managers of indigenous Somali nongovernmental organizations developed in the chaos of the early 1990s that deserve recognition and a place in the new power dispensation. Secularity and practical talent keep tradition and faith from becoming either anachronistic or blindly zealous.

The fourth element is the oracles and poets. Partly belonging to the traditional world of kin and religion but also cognizant of the potential of the future, the artistic community and its power of the aesthetic could be deployed to bring closer the traditional and the modern.

The fifth and final estate is Somali women. Severely marginalized by the patriarchal weight of Somali tradition and currently paying the greatest cost for the prevailing degeneration, Somali women will miss the past the least. More than any other segment of the society, their burning need for security, democratic life, material well-being, and respect and equality is a critical piece of the puzzle.

The militia leaders who arose in the aftermath of state breakdown may be a part of this group of authority figures needed to construct new institutions that can sustain a new political order. Their claims to authority, however, must be based upon more than access to guns and looted resources. Some of the militia leaders legitimately represent important constituencies and therefore can make the transition to political figures in a nonviolent setting. Others can only thrive in lawlessness and must be prevented from destroying a new order.

To get such a formulation moving and avoid a repetition of earlier miscalculations, consideration should be given to assembling these five groups along kin lines. Given the current breakdown of society into mutually suspicious and hostile clan fragments, reconstruction may need to begin from this base. The process may commence with the identification of elders who, in turn, would play a vital role in naming esteemed members of their respective communities to the other categories. If such a group, representing the most vital elements of Somali society could be assembled, it could begin the task of debating the great questions regarding the specific form and construction of a new Somali state.

Lessons for the International Community

The Somali crisis presented the international community with an early opportunity to develop strategies and mechanisms to address the political challenges of multilateral response to state collapse. The most distressing symptoms of the breakdown of institutions and political order in Somalia were the rampant lawlessness, factional fighting, and looting that generated famine, displacement, and massive violations of human rights including the loss of life. The abuse of the vulnerable by the vicious, however, was the manifestation of a deeper, fundamentally political problem. A sustainable solution that would make a return to the conditions of the humanitarian emergency less likely required addressing this underlying condition. Narrowly based operations designed to manage the humanitarian aspects alone are inadequate. The inherent nature of challenges like Somalia is fundamentally political and therefore a successful strategy must facilitate reconciliation and the reconstitution of institutions of legitimate political authority.

Building state institutions and the political structures necessary for a sustainable order is an immense and complex task. The further into anarchy a state descends, the more difficult the task becomes. Actions to prevent state collapse and to facilitate transitions from a political structure that can no longer sustain the state to a new order are critical to limiting the destruction. In Somalia, we outlined in chapter 3 a number of plausible opportunities where concerted international action in the waning years of Siad Barre's rule or in the early months following his departure might have halted the descent into complete collapse and thereby limited the degree of political reconciliation and institutional reconstruction necessary. There will always be cases, however, where lack of attention or miscalculation will lead to state collapse. The international community in the future undoubtedly will face the difficult and unwanted choices it faced regarding Somalia in November 1992.

Despite the insistence by policymakers in Washington that the goals of the international intervention were narrowly humanitarian, the operation had significant political consequences from the moment it was announced. As Somali actors tried to uncover how the deployment would affect their relative fortunes, they adopted responses that for good or ill shaped the framework for political reconciliation and the reestablishment of governing institutions. Every international action, from providing food to a famine region to meeting with factional leaders to sign a cease-fire, had unmistakable and often significant political repercussions.

In hindsight, it is possible to piece together and analyze two broad strategies that characterized most of the politically significant international actions, Accommodate Existing Forces and Encourage New Institutions. The first related to efforts to accommodate the existing armed groups into cease-fire agreements that would provide for a new regime composed of the militia chiefs. Efforts such as Ambassador Robert Oakley's cease-fire talks between warring factions in December 1992 and the UN-sponsored Addis Ababa talks of January and March 1993 are examples of actions that fall within this model. The second pattern, however, represented attempts to encourage new political leaders and institutions as the basis for a sustainable order. The law and order created by the presence of the international forces, the disarmament and encampment of some militia forces, the talks conducted by Oakley and others with representatives of civil society, and the efforts to include nonmilitia leaders in the institutions established by the March Addis Ababa meetings reflected this alternative strategy.

These two models of action, however, were in conflict because they arise from different assumptions regarding the nature of the underlying conditions. The accommodation strategy heartened the militia leaders while frightening some alternative leaders from civil society: the encouragement of new institutions strengthened nonmilitia elements but alarmed the armed groups that have the capacity to wreck any agreement. To pursue both simultaneously in the same area risks accomplishing neither.

The Addis Ababa agreement represented an attempt to combine these two strategies despite the inherent tension between them. The agreement had elements of both the Accommodate Existing Forces strategy in that it focused political power among the fourteen militia leaders. At the same time the agreements contained elements of the Encourage New Institutions strategy by including regional and district assemblies in the proposed political framework as a mechanism for nonmilitia participation. The agreement suggested a plan to encourage a shift in the international community's actions from short-term accommodation of the militias to a longer-term strategy of working with Somali civil society. The framework provided militia leaders with the opportunity to make the transition from "warlords" to "statesmen."

Owing in part to changes within the international operation's leadership, this agreement never received the full test it deserved. More important, the international community never committed itself to defending the agreement against attack from one or more of the forces that had a stake in preventing a new order. As analyzed above, it is not surprising that some of the organizations and militias initially accommodated by the international community could not or would not participate in a new order in which their power was sharply limited. The new institutions envisioned in the Addis Ababa agreements needed the security that could only come from the international forces to protect it from these destructive elements. In June 1993, the newborn institutions lacked the capacity, and the international operation lacked the commitment to stand up to the existing forces of disorder. When Mohamed Farah Aideed's Somali National Alliance decided to test the limits and attacked the UN peacekeepers, the fledgling new order collapsed into conflict.

A Final Note

As detailed in the narrative and analysis above, the Somali story is a tragedy on multiple levels for both the people of the region and the wider international community. These two sets of actors pursued their respective agendas with little recognition that they occupied the same stage and that achieving their goals required engaging each other. The Somalis could not break out of the vicious spiral of violence and destruction on their own in 1992. By the same token, the international community could not rebuild political institutions or manage the humanitarian emergency without local partners. The two sets of actors moved across the same stage with great drama and pathos from 1992 through 1994. Their failure to recognize that their fates required an appreciation of common purpose made the outcome a tragedy.

Appendix A

Models of Political Strategies

As discussed in chapter 4, intervention in Somalia by the international community was based on two implicit strategies, labeled Accommodate Existing Forces and Encourage New Institutions. One of the most important lessons from an analysis of the Somali intervention is that the implications of these models and the manner in which they interact may be critical to the success of a political strategy. This appendix therefore considers the implications of these models in a more conceptual manner, building on the empirical findings in Somalia but deriving more general inferences (see figure A-1).

Accommodate Existing Forces

The Accommodate Existing Forces strategy is based on a judgment (whether explicit or implicit) that the forces that survived or developed following state collapse represent the principal source of legitimate authority and therefore should be the core of a new, sustainable order. The international interveners therefore may seek to encourage a generalized cease-fire and power-sharing arrangement among these forces. In some cases a single force or alliance will be capable of serving as the core of a new order, and the goal of the external actors can be to encourage the consolidation of its power.[1] If multilateral forces are needed they may operate according to traditional UN peacekeeping doctrine, maintaining neutrality and relying on the consent of the local authorities before deployment. If the forces that survived state collapse are capable of acting as the basis for a new, sustainable order based on legitimate authority, the intervention may be minimized in time, money, and risk.

70

Figure A-1 Two Models of Political Strategies

| | Strategies | |
| | Accommodate | Encourage new |
Conditions	existing forces	institutions
Underlying conditions	Forces that developed or survived state collapse and anarchy capable of serving as basis for new enduring order.	Existing institutions not capable of forming new order. Need to encourage alternative structures.
Imagining political reconciliation	Balance of power among militias. Most important social organizations represented by militias.	New institutions and leaders develop when security in place. Militia leaders encouraged to participate as political figures.
Operational implications	Traditional peacekeeping operations, modified for the lack of an agreement, are possible. Short time frame, no disarmament.	Security umbrella with more determined intervention. Longer term, more costly, and intrusive.

Underlying Conditions

In conditions of anarchy where other institutions such as political parties, unions, professional groups, women's associations, and other components of civil society have been shattered, militias may be the principal form in which local people have organized themselves. If the military leaders are supported by a broad constituency attracted by the ability of their organization to provide assistance and protection, and the militias have the ability to transform themselves into political organizations capable of maintaining that support under peaceful conditions, then they may serve as the basis for a new order. Besides their position as the major institutions that exist following state collapse, the militias have the ability to disrupt any agreement that they do not support. Under these conditions, therefore, getting an agreement among the militias is the paramount goal of political reconciliation.

Imagining Political Reconciliation

Under such conditions, the international community's intervention may follow well-established UN Chapter VI doctrine and accept all militia commanders as legitimate political leaders. The intervention therefore would not try to alter the make-up of organizations but would encourage an end to hostilities among existing warring parties. The political goal under such a strategy might be to establish a broadly inclusive balance of power among the militias so that no one group could dominate. Such a settlement would convince those with the arms capable of disrupting any settlement to perceive an agreement as serving their interests. To win broad support from militia leaders, accountability for past behavior and human rights abuses that took place during the chaotic period of conflict may have to be deemphasized.[2]

Operational Implications

When the forces that survived state collapse are capable of serving as the building blocks of a new order and the strategy of the international intervention is to accommodate these forces and facilitate an agreement among them, an intervention similar to a traditional UN peacekeeping operation may be possible. No major actions or deployments would take place without the consent of local forces. Disarmament, unless agreed to by all factions, would be avoided. The time frame could be relatively short and the risk of casualties relatively low. The armed groups that grew up following the collapse of the state will be more likely to cooperate with the international operation and its political strategy if they perceive that it will allow them to preserve their power and perquisites.

The nature of state collapse, however, will require some flexibility and creativity to make peacekeeping effective and relevant to the challenges at hand. Rather than starting with a cease-fire, the intervening forces will have to work in conjunction with diplomatic initiatives to broker an agreement. Depending on the circumstances and the activities of the intervening forces, their presence may hinder or promote the search for such a cessation of hostilities. One of the strengths of traditional UN peacekeeping operations is its neutrality. The international force therefore should make extraordinary efforts to avoid conflict with any of the local forces.

Encourage New Institutions

The Encourage New Institutions model, in contrast, arises from a contrasting set of conclusions about the nature of the organizations that developed following state collapse. In some circumstances, these forces cannot act as the basis of a new sustainable order. Rather than deriving their influence from legitimate authority, as determined by the local population, these groups have seized power by force of arms, looting, and intimidation. To be sustainable, the new political order must tap into the sources of legitimacy within the underlying society. To encourage these new leaders and limit the intimidation of those forces with an interest in continuing instability, the multilateral intervention may need to provide a "security umbrella" that will allow new institutions to develop. When the existing organizations cannot act as the basis for a new order, traditional UN peacekeeping doctrine will need to be expanded and more expansive mandates put in place.

Underlying Conditions

An alternative way of understanding the political context in the aftermath of state collapse is to conclude that the militia leaders are a major source of instability rather than the basis of a new political order. Some of the forces that thrived in the Hobbesian chaos can not survive the transition to peace and security and therefore have a stake in subverting reconciliation. Such groups will have to be transformed or marginalized for order to return and endure.

Militia leaders in many cases do not create anarchy accidentally but rather thrive as a direct consequence of the population's insecurity. The absence of the law and order allowed them to thrive regardless of their legitimacy in the eyes of the terrorized population. The fact that a militia leader is capable of fielding a significant force in a context of anarchy is not by itself evidence of his legitimacy. Said S. Samatar, a Somali historian, described the basis of support for a Somali militia chief: "Only so long as he can lead looters to the next village for booty can he count on their [his followers] support. The moment he is deprived of the power to raid, his opportunistic followers are likely to desert him."[3] In Serbia as well, observers have noted that "Milosevic counted on war, the ultimate condition of fear, to unite Serbs around him."[4]

State collapse and societal collapse are intertwined. When governing institutions disappear, social structures are distorted if not crushed by the additional pressures. Without the state to provide protection, security, and access to the means of survival, people turn to other institutions such as the ethnic group, church, mosque, temple, clan, and family. Some social institutions thrive, others collapse with the state. In any event, regardless of the trauma and violence that has distorted civil society and forced many of its leaders into hiding, with time and an appropriate enabling environment, leaders and organizations responsive to local needs and representing authority that is legitimate in local eyes may emerge.

Imagining Political Reconciliation

When the militias are not capable of serving as the means to a future order, the international intervention may need to consider special measures to encourage alternative leaders to step forward. Rules to identify nascent or underground leaders who are locally legitimate and effective are few. The process of addressing collective grievances, selecting legitimate spokespersons, forging and reforging social alliances, and eventually creating local and national organizations takes time, and the outcome cannot be determined in advance.[5] The critical ingredients to this kind of political reconciliation are security and time. A security umbrella provided by international intervention enables the "silent majority" previously threatened and mistreated by the militia leaders, to come forward to build institutions and political authority capable of managing a new order.[6]

Militia leaders should be given the option of joining the peace and state-building process as leaders of constituencies, whether clan based or otherwise defined. Some may be able to make the transition from military to civilian leadership and should be encouraged. Others can only survive and keep their organizations operating in conditions of warfare and chaos with the opportunities these conditions provide for looting and terrorizing. These true "warlords" must be prevented from playing a spoiler's role, and the international community needs the force, rules of engagement, and political will to isolate any who attempt to disrupt the process by throwing the country back into violence.

Operational Implications

Under this scenario, the international community undertakes a difficult task under difficult circumstances: engage in political reconciliation and state building in the absence of an agreement among the warring factions on a political framework. Clearly it is easier and preferable to conduct humanitarian operations without the burden of state building, but in cases of state collapse that option is unavailable. Similarly, it is easier to engage in state building once there is an agreement among the warring factions but, again, sometimes that option is not available.

An effort to encourage new political leaders to step forward will require more time than many international decisionmakers want to accept at present. Rather than sanctioning the swift use of overwhelming force followed by a quick withdrawal, decisionmakers must use international forces as part of a more measured and patient strategy. A large fighting force that may be necessary in the initial phase to stabilize the situation, intimidate any local forces considering resisting the intervention, and provide security for the humanitarian operations may be replaced fairly quickly by a much smaller force armed and trained to perform more like police forces. A significant fighting force may be necessary on short notice, and some rapid deployment units may stay near the region for an extended period. However, a well-constructed operation should not require sustained combat. Some forces, such as those from the United States, are better equipped and trained to perform the first task, while other states take on the second. What matters is that the deployment of force relate to a strategy of long-term political reconciliation.

Militarily, the objective of enforcement operations is to minimize the use of force against civilian groups rather than to defeat a rival force. As John G. Ruggie put it, "The political objective of using international force to neutralize local force is to prevent local force from becoming the arbiter of outcomes, and to speed up the process whereby the local combatants become persuaded that they have no viable alternative but to reach a negotiated political settlement."[7]

Reasonable efforts to reduce the availability of weapons and end the use of force for political purposes may be appropriate, although total disarmament clearly is impossible. After a lengthy period of anarchy during which personal weapons were critical to survival, the local population will consider it more prudent to hide their weapons rather than allow themselves to be disarmed. Because total disarmament is not feasible, the key aim of the international forces and a future local interim administration must be to create a political and economic climate in which buried guns stay buried. Aldo Ajello, the UN special representative in charge of the operation in Mozambique realistically appraised the options: "I know very well that they will give us old and obsolete matériel, and they will have here and there something hidden. I don't care. What I do is create the political situation in which the use of those guns is not the question. So that they stay where they are."[8]

It may well be advisable and feasible, however, to reduce the quantity and quality of weapons by seizing unregistered guns, forcing encampment of large weapons, and regulating where and when weapons may be possessed.

Multiple Strategies

The conclusion that different strategies are appropriate for different conditions raises other questions. In Somalia and other cases of state collapse, different conditions existed in different geographical regions of the old state. The forces that survived state collapse in one geographic region may be capable of serving as the building blocks for a new, sustainable order while the forces in another part of the same state may not. An Accommodate Existing Forces strategy may be appropriate for a region like northwestern or northeastern Somalia, for example, while an Encourage New Institutions strategy may be needed in regions like southern Somalia. The former strategy clearly is preferable to the latter because the international community should limit its interference to the minimum necessary.

Besides the need to adjust political objectives, operational doctrine and even mandates to correspond to varying conditions, the international strategy must be flexible enough to change as dynamics on the ground are transformed. Many local actors inevitably will change their character over time in response to the incentives and constraints imposed by the intervention. In the early stages of an intervention, the operational requirements of deployment will probably require an initial tactic of working with the existing powers, implicitly following the Accommodating Existing Forces framework. Over time, however, the political strategy must consider making the transition to an Encouraging New Institutions model in order to put in place a sustainable new order based on locally legitimate forms of authority. Only by keeping this longer-term goal in mind can the international community play a constructive part in promoting political reconciliation following state collapse.

Appendix B

Major Somali Movements[1]

The following factions participated in one or more of the January, March, and November 1993 meetings in Addis Ababa. Several organizations are listed twice, with different leaderships; these are factions that were split internally (usually along subclan lines) but that have chosen not to rename their movements. The frequency of shifts in factional and clan alliances means that portions of this list are already out of date.

In the Addis Ababa meetings, two loose coalitions were created: The Somali Salvation Alliance (SSA), led by Ali Mahdi, and the Somali National Alliance (SNA), led by Aideed.

Somali African Muki Organization (SAMO)—Represents minority populations of Bantu origin in the southern riverine regions, the most vulnerable victims of the war and famine. One faction was allied with the Somali Salvation Alliance and another was allied with the Somali National Alliance.

Somali Democratic Alliance (SDA)—A Gadabursi (Dir clan) organization from the northern "Somaliland" region around Boroma. Originally formed in 1989, it opposed the SNM's policy of independence and participated in the Addis Ababa talks. Allied with the SSA.

Somali Democratic Movement (SDM)—The SDM, an organization based among the Rahanwein people (the agriculturalists of Somalia who suffered some of the worse consequences of the famine), active around the town of Baidoa, split and reformed a number of times in 1992–94. At different times various factions have been associated with both the SSA and the SNA.

Somali National Democratic Union (SNDU)—A Darod faction allied with the SSA.

Somali National Front (SNF)—Led by General Omar Haji Mohamed Siad Hersi "Morgan," the SNF was composed of Marehan (part of the Darod and Siad Barre's clan) and was allied with the SSA.

Somali National Movement (SNM)—An Isaq-based movement that led the opposition to Siad Barre in the late 1980s. The SNM was formed in 1981 and was supported by Ethiopia during much of the 1980s. In 1988 the SNM occupied much of northern Somalia and suffered brutal attacks from Siad Barre. The SNM won control over the north (former British Somaliland) in 1991 and declared the territory the independent (but as yet unrecognized) Republic of Somaliland.

Somali National Union (SNU)—This Reer-Hamar group is supported by many coastal, urban Somalis. Historically these urbanized groups have had weak clan links to the rest of Somalia but strong trading links to the Indian Ocean. As a relatively wealthy minority, they suffered greatly during the civil war and banditry. Different factions of the SNU have been allied with the SSA and SNA.

Somali Patriotic Movement (SPM)—This grouping of Ogadeni subclans (of the Darod clan) has attempted to lay claim to the region around the southern port of Kismayu, thereby triggering conflict with other Ogadeni subclans. One faction was led by Ahmed Omar Jess and was allied with Aideed's SNA. Another faction led by Adan Abdullahi Nur "Gabiyo" was allied with Ali Mahdi's SSA and with General Mohamed Siad Hersi "Morgan."

Somali Salvation Democratic Front (SSDF)—Led by General Mohamed Abshir Musse and supported by many Mijerteen (of the Darod clan), its regional stronghold is northeastern Somalia. It was formed in 1979 by Colonel Yusuf Abdullahi following Siad Barre's attacks on the Mijerteen and supported by Ethiopia in the 1980s. Tensions with Aideed led the SSDF generally to side with the Ali Mahdi's SSA. A smaller SSDF group is based in Kismayu among the Herti subclan and has fought with the SPM faction under Colonel Jess. The movement underwent a complicated leadership struggle in late 1994.

Southern Somali National Movement (SSNM)—This Dir clan movement is based among the Bimaal subclan in southern coastal Somalia. It is split between factions, one allied with Aideed's SNA, another with Ali Mahdi's SSA.

United Somali Congress (USC)—This group, with support among the Hawiye, seized control of Mogadishu in 1991. The USC split into two sub-clan-based factions. The faction, allied with the SNA is led by General Mohammed Farah "Aideed" and many of the Habir Gedir subclan. It maintained control over southern Mogadishu and some regions in central Somalia. The faction allied with the SSA is led by "interim president" Ali Mahdi Mohamed and many of the Abgal subclan, maintaining control of northern Mogadishu.

United Somali Front (USF)—An Issa group (Dir clan) based in the far northwest (Somaliland). The Issa broke with the SNM in 1991 and has had close relations with the government of Djibouti. Loosely allied with the SSA.

United Somali Party (USP)—A Dolbahante-Warsangali subclan (of the Darod clan) movement. This subclan straddles the border between northern Somaliland and southern Somalia, and the USP has been in conflict with the SNM. Allied with the SSA.

Notes

Chapter One

1. I. William Zartman, "Introduction: Posing the Problem of State Collapse," in I. William Zartman, ed., *Collapsed States: The Disintegration and Restoration of Legitimate Authority* (Boulder: Lynne Rienner, 1995). For an earlier statement see Aristide R. Zolberg, "The Specter of Anarchy: African States Verging on Dissolution," *Dissent*, vol. 39 (Summer 1992), pp. 303–11.

2. Robert Kaplan, "The Coming Anarchy," *Atlantic Monthly*, vol. 273 (February 1994), p. 45.

3. Kenichi Ohmae, "The Rise of the Region State," *Foreign Affairs*, vol. 72 (Spring 1993), pp. 78–87

4. Zartman, "Introduction: Posing the Problem of State Collapse," in Zartman, ed., *Collapsed States: The Disintegration and Restoration of Legitimate Authority.* For a picture of what this looks like from the ground see John Darnton, "Zaire Drifting into Anarchy as Authority Disintegrates," *New York Times*, May 24, 1994, p. A1.

5. Crawford Young, "The Dialectics of Cultural Pluralism: Concept and Reality," in Crawford Young, ed., *The Rising Tide of Cultural Pluralism: The Nation-State at Bay?* (University of Wisconsin Press, 1993), p. 3.

6. For a discussion of these norms in the African state system see Crawford Young, "Self-Determination, Territorial Integrity, and the African State System," in Francis M. Deng and I. William Zartman, eds., *Conflict Resolution in Africa* (Brookings, 1991), pp. 320–46.

7. J. Samuel Barkin and Bruce Cronin, "The State and the Nation: Changing Norms and the Rules of Sovereignty in International Relations," *International Organization*, vol. 48 (Winter 1994), p. 108.

8. Francis M. Deng and Larry Minear, *The Challenges of Famine Relief: Emergency Operations in the Sudan* (Brookings, 1992), p. 124.

9. Boutros Boutros-Ghali, *An Agenda for Peace: Preventive Diplomacy, Peacemaking, and Peace-keeping* (New York: United Nations, 1992), p. 9. For other views see Thomas G. Weiss and Jarat Chopra, "Sovereignty Is No Longer Sacrosanct: Codifying Humanitarian Intervention," *Ethics and International Affairs*,

vol. 6 (1992), pp. 95–117; and David J. Scheffer, "Toward a Modern Doctrine of Humanitarian Intervention," *University of Toledo Law Review*, vol. 23 (Winter 1992), pp. 253–93.

10. Thomas G. Weiss and Larry Minear, "Preface," in Thomas G. Weiss and Larry Minear, *Humanitarianism across Borders: Sustaining Civilians in Times of War* (Boulder: Lynne Rienner, 1993), p. vii. The Humanitarianism and War Project, which produced this volume, has contributed much of the most innovative thinking on these questions.

11. Stanley Hoffmann, "Avoiding New World Disorder," *New York Times*, February 25, 1991, p. A19.

12. Francis M. Deng, *Protecting the Dispossessed: A Challenge for the International Community* (Brookings, 1993); and Gerald B. Helman and Steven R. Ratner, "Saving Failed States," *Foreign Policy*, no. 89 (Winter 92–93), pp. 3–20.

13. Paul Harrison and Robin Palmer, *News Out of Africa: Biafra to Band Aid* (London: Hillary Shipman, 1986); Edward Girardet, "Public Opinion, the Media, and Humanitarianism," in Weiss and Minear, *Humanitarianism across Borders*, pp. 39–55; Stephen Hess, "Crisis, TV, and Public Pressure," *Brookings Review*, vol. 12 (Winter 1994), p. 48; Christopher J. Bosso, "Setting the Agenda: Mass Media and the Discovery of Famine in Ethiopia," in Michael Margolis and Gary A. Mauser, eds., *Manipulating Public Opinion: Essays of Public Opinion as a Dependent Variable* (Pacific Grove, Calif.: Brooks/Cole, 1989), pp. 153–74; Nik Gowing, "Behind the CNN Factor: Lights! Camera! Attrocities! but Policy Makers Swear They're Not Swayed by TV Images," editorial, *Washington Post*, July 31, 1994, p. C1; and Michael Maren, "Feeding a Famine," *Media Critic*, vol. 2 (Fall 1994), pp. 30–38.

14. J. Brian Atwood, "Suddenly, Chaos," Washington Post, July 31, 1994, p. C9. See also J. Brian Atwood, "From the Cold War to Chaos and Cholera," *New Perspectives Quarterly*, vol. 11 (Fall 1994), pp. 21–22.

15. Lester B. Pearson, "Force for the U.N.," *Foreign Affairs*, vol. 35 (April 1957), p. 401. See also Henry Wiseman, "Peacekeeping in the International Political Context: Historical Analysis and Future Directions," in Indar Jit Rikhye and Kjell Skjelsbaek, eds., *The United Nations and Peacekeeping: Results, Limitations and Prospects* (London: Macmillan for the International Peace Academy, 1990), pp. 32–51.

16. Marrack Goulding, "The Evolution of United Nations Peacekeeping," *International Affairs*, vol. 69 (1993), pp. 451–64; and Boutros Boutros-Ghali, "UN Peace-Keeping in a New Era: A New Chance for Peace," *World Today*, vol. 49 (April 1993), p. 67.

17. Paul F. Diehl, *International Peacekeeping* (Johns Hopkins University Press, 1993), p. 13. For similar definitions see Marrack Goulding, "The Evolution of United Nations Peacekeeping," *International Affairs*, vol. 69 (1993), p. 455; Brian Urquhart, "Beyond the 'Sheriff's Posse,'" *Survival*, vol. 32 (May–June 1990), p. 198; The United Nations, *The Blue Helmets: A Review of United Nations Peacekeeping*, 2d ed. (New York: United Nations Department of Public Information, 1990), pp. 4–5.

18. Ernest W. Lefever, *Crisis in the Congo: A United Nations Force in Action* (Brookings, 1965).

19. Lawrence Freedman and David Boren, "'Safe Havens' for Kurds in Post-War Iraq" in Nigel Rodley, ed., *To Loose the Bands of Wickedness: International Intervention in Defence of Human Rights* (London, 1992), pp. 43–92.

20. For some accounts on proposals for new UN roles see John Mackinlay and Jarat Chopra, "Second Generation Multilateral Operations," *Washington Quarterly*, vol. 15 (Summer 1992), p. 113; Marrack Goulding, "The Evolution of United Nations Peacekeeping," *International Affairs*, vol. 68 (1993), pp. 451–64; Augustus R. Norton and Thomas G. Weiss, "Superpowers and Peace-Keepers," *Survival*, vol. 32 (May–June 1990), pp. 212–13; and George L. Sherry, *The United Nations Reborn: Conflict Control in the Post–Cold War World* (New York: Council on Foreign Relations, 1990), pp. 26–29.

21. Brian E. Urquhart, "Reflections by the Chairman," in Rikhye and Skjelsbaek, *The United Nations and Peacekeeping*, p. 17.

22. Stanley Meisler, "Dateline U.N.: A New Hammarskjold?" *Foreign Policy*, no. 98 (Spring 1995), p. 188.

23. Ernst B. Haas, "Collective Conflict Management: Evidence for a New World Order?" in Thomas G. Weiss, ed., *Collective Security in a Changing World* (Boulder: Lynne Rienner, 1992), pp. 74–75. See also Johan Kaufmann and Nico Schrijver, *Changing Global Needs: Expanding Roles for the United Nations System* (Hanover,N.H.: Academic Council on the United Nations System, 1990), pp. 77–88.

24. Brian Urquhart, "Who Can Stop Civil Wars?" *New York Times*, December 29, 1991, sec. 4, p. 9.

25. Brian Urquhart, "Who Can Police the World?" *New York Review of Books*, May 12, 1994, p. 29.

26. Recent evaluations of the UN mission in Cambodia, however, are considerably more mixed. See William Branigin, "Ambitious U.N. Effort in Cambodia Left Country with Old Problems," *Washington Post*, August 26, 1994, p. A19.

27. Mats R. Berdal, *Whither UN Peacekeeping?*, Adelphi Paper 281 (London: International Institute for Strategic Studies, October 1993), contains a number of thoughtful warnings about excessive expectations of UN peacekeeping.

28. Ernst B. Haas, "Beware the Slippery Slope: Notes toward the Definition of Justifiable Intervention," in Laura W. Reed and Carl Kaysen, eds., *Emerging Norms of Justified Intervention* (Cambridge, Mass.: American Academy of Arts and Sciences, 1993), p. 65. See also Mats R. Berdal, "Fateful Encounter: The United States and UN Peacekeeping," *Survival*, vol. 36 (Spring 1994), p. 30.

29. Stephen John Stedman, "The New Interventionists," *Foreign Affairs*, vol. 72 (January–February 1993), p. 8.

Chapter Two

1. The classic account of Somali society is I.M. Lewis, *A Pastoral Democracy: A Study of Pastoralism and Politics among the Northern Somalis of the Horn of Africa* (Oxford University Press, 1961). See also I.M. Lewis, *A Modern History of Somalia* (Boulder: Westview, 1988); and David Laitin and Said Samatar, *Somalia: Nation in Search of a State* (Boulder: Westview, 1987).

2. Ahmed Samatar, "The Curse of Allah: Civic Disembowelment and the Collapse of the State in Somalia," in Ahmed I. Samatar, ed., *The Somali Challenge: From Catastrophe to Renewal?* (Boulder: Lynne Rienner, 1994), pp. 109–11.

3. On *heer* see Maxamed D. Afrax, "The Mirror of Culture: Somali Dissolution Seen Through Oral Expression," in Samatar, ed., *The Somali Challenge*, pp. 236–37.

4. For a similar analysis see Patricia Crone, "The Tribe and the State," in John A. Hall, ed., *States in History* (Cambridge: Basil Blackwell, 1986).

5. A.I. Samatar, *Socialist Somalia: Rhetoric and Reality* (London: Zed, 1988).

6. Abdi Samatar, Lance Salisbury, and Jonathan Bascom, "The Political Economy of Livestock Marketing in Northern Somalia," *African Economic History*, vol. 17 (1988), pp. 81–97; and Abdi Samatar, "The Demise of Somali Traditions: The Politics of Development and Reform," *Proceedings: 3rd International Conference on the Horn of Africa* (New York: City College of New York, 1988).

7. That actions by many officials were a cause for concern, see the beautiful *gabay* (poetry) of the late Abdillahi Sultan, "Timaaday"—a hero of the independence movement in the north and one of the greatest Somali poets in this century. See Boobe Yusuf Dualeh, *Maansadii Timacadde* (Mogadishu, 1983).

8. Ozay Mahmet, "Effectiveness of Foreign Aid: The Somali Case," *Journal of Modern African Studies*, vol. 9 (May 1971), pp. 31–47.

9. Samatar, *Socialist Somalia*, p. 67.

10. I. M. Lewis, *A Modern History of Somalia: Nation and State in the Horn of Africa* (Boulder: Westview, 1985), p. 204.

11. Lewis, *A Modern History*, pp. 205–06.

12. For example, the collection of blood payments by clans for offenses was made illegal. Instead of identifying themselves by their clan affiliation, Somalis began to talk of their "ex-clans." See I. M. Lewis, "The Ogaden and the Fragility of Somali Segmentary Nationalism," *African Affairs*, vol. 88 (October 1991), p. 573.

13. I. M. Lewis, "Kim Il-Sung in Somalia: End of Tribalism?" in William A. Shack and Percy S. Cohen, eds., *Politics in Leadership* (Oxford: Clarendon Press, 1979), pp. 13–44.

14. Terrence Lyons, "The Horn of Africa Regional Politics," in W. Howard Wriggins, ed., *Dynamics of Regional Politics: Four Systems on the Indian Ocean Rim* (Columbia University Press, 1992), pp. 155–209.

15. I.M. Lewis, "The Ogaden and the Fragility of Somali Segmentary Nationalism," *African Affairs*, vol. 88 (October 1991).

16. Abdi Samatar, "Social Class and Economic Restructuring in Pastoral Africa: Notes from Somalia," *African Studies Review*, vol. 35 (April 1992).

17. Farzin suggests two reasons: badly coordinated and ill-prepared food aid by donors; and "imprudent" state actions that favor urban consumers at the expense of producers. Y. Hossein Farzin, *Food Import Dependence in Somalia: Magnitude, Causes, and Policy Options* (Washington: World Bank, 1988). See also United Nations Development Program, *Somalia: Annual Development Cooperation Report, 1987* (Mogadishu: UNDP, September 1988).

18. One measure of the precipitous decline of incomes in Somalia is evidenced

by trends in real official minimum wages. If 1980 is taken as 100, by 1985–86 this figure has contracted to an unbearable low of 22. See Dharan Ghai, "Economic Growth, Structural Change and Labour Absorption in Africa: 1960–86," UN Research Institute for Social Development Discussion Paper 1(Geneva, 1987).

19. For example, the balance of payments of Somalia in 1985, 1986, and 1988 ran a deficit of around $220 million, $371 million, and $380 million respectively. The final figure is nearly five times the export earnings. *African Recovery*, vol.3 (October 1989), p. 27.

20. Abdi Samatar, "Social Class and Economic Restructuring in Pastoral Africa: Notes from Somalia," *African Studies Review*, vol. 35 (April 1992), pp. 101–27.

21. One of the ways which Somali regimes have done this is through foreign assistance. In 1986, nearly all of Somalia's development expenditures were coming from this source. See Abdi Samatar, *The State and Rural Transformation in Northern Somalia, 1884–1986* (University of Wisconsin Press, 1989), p. 149. See also Albert L. Gray, Jr., "The Economy of the Somali Democratic Republic in the 1980s," *Ufahamu*, vol.17 (Spring 1989), pp. 128–30.

22. Abdi Samatar, "Structural Adjustment as Development Strategy in the Third World: Bananas, Boom, and Poverty in Somalia," *Economic Geography*, vol. 69 (1993), pp. 117–31.

23. The infant mortality rate for 1987 was 151 per 1,000 live births; access to drinking water was available for 11 percent of the population; and education had a budget allocation of 2 percent of total government expenditures. For more, see United Nations Development Program (UNDP), *Somalia: Annual Development Cooperation Report* (Mogadishu, 1988).

24. The 1987–88 aid commitments to Somalia were estimated at $360 million (at 1986 prices and exchange rates), of which a significant part would go to feed refugees. Ibid., p. 10.

25. "Africa's Debt Profile: 1989," *African Recovery*, vol. 4 (October–December 1990), p.93. Somali total debt was $2.137 billion, most to multilateral creditors and foreign governments. Debt service payments in 1989 were more than 124 percent of export earnings.

26. In fact, much of the support came from the Omar Mohamoud subclan of the Mijerteen. Some other subclans refused to get involved with the Somali Salavation Democratic Front.

27. The SNM drew considerable support from the Isaq diaspora working in the Gulf. For details see Christopher Clapham, "The Political Economy of Conflict in the Horn of Africa," *Survival*, vol. 32 (September–October 1990), pp. 403–20.

28. For details, see *Agreement on Normalization of Relations between The Somali Democratic Republic and The People's Democratic Republic of Ethiopia* (April 3, 1988). See "Somalia: Under Fire," *Africa Confidential*, April 29, 1988.

29. "Somali Government Accused in 50,000 Civilian Deaths," *Africa Report* (March–April 1990), p. 10. See also the report written for the Department of State. Robert Gersony, *Why Somalis Flee: Synthesis of Accounts of Conflict Experienced in Northern Somalia by Somali Refugees, Displaced Persons and Others* (Department of State, Bureau for Refugee Programs, August 1989).

30. Daniel Compagnon, "The Somali Opposition Fronts: Some Comments and Questions," *Horn of Africa*, vol.13 (January–June 1990), pp. 36–37.

31. Amnesty International, *Somalia: A Long-Term Human Rights Crisis* (London: Amnesty International Publications, September 1988).

32. "Kenya: Forcible Return of Somali Refugees and Government Repression of Kenya Somalis," *News from Africa Watch*, press release, November 17, 1989, p. 2.

33. Charles L. Geshekter, "The Death of Somalia in Historical Perspective," in Mary E. Morris and Emile Sahliyeh, eds., *Unity vs. Separatism in the Middle East* (Santa Monica, Calif.: Rand, forthcoming).

34. David D. Laitin and Said S. Samatar, *Somalia: Nation in Search of a State* (Boulder: Westview, 1987), pp. 93–94.

35. See Osman Mohamoud, "Somalia: Crisis and Decay in an Authoritarian Regime," *Horn of Africa*, vol. 4 (September 1981), p. 11. An interesting list of the top state positions assigned to the president's relatives is found in "Documentary Evidence of the Clan-Base of the Current Regime," *Somali Horizon*, vol. 9 (October–September–December 1987), pp. 16–17.

36. Said Samatar, *Somalia: A Nation in Turmoil* (London: Minority Rights Group Report, August 1991). For a detailed early account see Daniel Compagnon, "The Somali Opposition Fronts: Some Comments and Questions," *Horn of Africa*, vol.13 (January–June 1990), pp. 29–54.

37. Hussein M. Adam, "Somalia: Militarism, Warlordism or Democracy?" *Review of African Political Economy*, no. 54 (July 1992), pp. 11–26.

38. Daniel Compagnon, "The Somali Opposition Fronts: Some Comments and Questions," *Horn of Africa*, vol.13 (January–June 1990), pp. 29–54. See also "Rebuilding Snagged by Divisions," *Africa News*, vol. 34 (February 11, 1991), p. 9. "Somalia: A Friend in Need," *Africa Confidential*, December 7, 1990, pp. 6–7; and Hussein Adam, "Somalia: A Terrible Beauty Being Born?" in I. William Zartman, ed., *Collapsed States: The Disintegration and Restoration of Legitimate Authority* (Boulder: Lynne Rienner, 1995).

39. Amnesty International, *Somalia: Report on an Amnesty International Visit and Current Human Rights Concerns* (London: Amnesty International, January 1990), p. 5.

40. Amnesty International, *Somalia: Report on an International Visit*, pp. 4–5; Amnesty International, *Somalia: Extrajudicial Executions* (London: Amnesty International, June 1990); and Neil Henry, "Massacre in Somalia Spurred Shift in U.S. Policy," *Washington Post*, February 19, 1990, p. A21.

41. Amnesty International, *Somalia: Extrajudicial Executions*, p. 5.

42. Neil Henry, "Rebels, Rights Groups Attack Somalia," *Washington Post*, February 18, 1990, p. A23.

43. Neil Henry, "Somalia Orders Trial for Signers of Rights Letter," *Washington Post*, July 14, 1990, p. A20; and Mohamed Osman Omar, *The Road to Zero: Somalia's Self-Destruction* (London: Haan, 1992), pp. 196–99.

44. "The Mayor of Mogdishu." *Economist*, September 29, 1990, p. 47.

45. Hussein Adam, "Somalia: Militarism, Warlordism or Democracy?" *Review of Africa Political Economy*, no. 54 (July 1992), p. 21. On this period of urban terror

see also Ali K. Galaydh, "Notes on the State of the Somali State," *Horn of Africa*, vol. 13 (January–June 1990), pp. 24–27.

46. "In Somalia, Graves and Devastation," *New York Times*, January 30, 1991, p. A2.

47. Ken Menkhaus and Terrence Lyons, "What Are the Lessons to Be Learned from Somalia?" *CSIS Africa Notes*, no. 144 (Washington: Center for Strategic and International Studies, 1993).

48. Menkhaus and Lyons, "What Are the Lessons to Be Learned?" p. 3.

49. Jeffrey Clark, "Debacle in Somalia: Failure of the Collective Response," in Lori Fisler Damrosch, ed., *Enforcing Restraint: Collective Intervention in Internal Conflicts* (New York: Council on Foreign Relations, 1993), p. 211.

50. Africa Watch, "Somalia: A Fight to the Finish?" *News from Africa Watch*, vol. 4 (February 13,1992), p. 7.

51. Ahmed I. Samatar, "The Curse of Allah: Civic Disembowelment and the Collapse of the State in Somalia," in Ahmed I. Samatar, ed., *The Somali Challenge: From Catastrophe to Renewal?* (Boulder: Lynne Rienner, 1994), pp. 122–25.

52. Menkhaus and Lyons, "What Are the Lessons to Be Learned?"

Chapter Three

1. In particular, Rakiya Omaar and Alex De Waal of the human rights organization Africa Watch documented conditions in great detail and contextual understanding. See, for example, "Somalia: Human Rights Abuses and Civil War in the North," *News from Africa Watch*, press release, July 21, 1989; and "Somalia: An Update on Human Rights Developments since Mid-July," *News from Africa* Watch, press release, September 22, 1989.

2. Terrence Lyons, "Great Powers and Conflict Reduction in the Horn of Africa," in I. William Zartman, ed., *Cooperative Security: Reducing Third World Wars* (Syracuse University Press, 1995); Robert G. Patman, *The Soviet Union in the Horn of Africa: The Diplomacy of Intervention and Disengagement* (Cambridge: Cambridge University Press, 1990); and Paul B. Henze, *The Horn of Africa: From War to Peace* (St. Martin's Press, 1991).

3. Jeffrey A. Lefebvre, *Arms for the Horn: U.S. Security Policy in Ethiopia and Somalia, 1953–1991* (University of Pittsburgh Press, 1991), p. 241.

4. Wolfgang Achtner, "The Italian Connection: How Rome Helped Ruin Somalia," *Washington Post*, January 24, 1993, p. C3; and Giampaolo Calchi Novati, "Italy in the Triangle of the Horn: Too Many Corners for a Half Power," *Journal of Modern African Studies*, vol. 32 (September 1994), pp. 369–86.,

5. David Rawson, "Dealing with Disintegration: U.S. Assistance and the Somali State," in Ahmed I. Samatar, ed., *The Somali Challenge: From Catastrophe to Renewal?* (Boulder: Lynne Rienner, 1994).

6. U.S. House of Representatives, Subcommittee on Africa, *Reported Massacres and Indiscriminate Killings in Somalia*, July 14, 1988, 100 Cong., 2d sess.(Government Printing Office, 1989). See particularly the testimony by Aryeh Neier, vice chair of Human Rights Watch. Congressional criticism of Somalia's human rights record

froze funding and the embassy finally began reducing its presence following the June 1989 riots and massacres in Mogadishu. See Rawson, "Dealing with Disintegration," pp. 175–76; and Lefebvre, *Arms for the Horn*, pp. 242–44.

7. Mohamed Sahnoun, *Somalia: The Missed Opportunities* (Washington: U.S. Institute of Peace, 1994), p. xiii.

8. Robert Gersony, *Why Somalis Flee: Synthesis of Accounts of Conflict Experience in Northern Somalia by Somali Refugees, Displaced Persons and Others* (Department of State, Bureau for Refugee Programs, August 1989), pp. 60–61.

9. Novati, "Italy in the Triangle of the Horn: Too Many Corners for a Half Power."

10. U.S. General Accounting Office, *Somalia: Observations Regarding the Northern Conflict and Resulting Conditions, 4 May 1989* (Washington, 1990); and U.S. General Accounting Office, *Somalia: U.S. Strategic Interests and Assistance* (Washington, February 1990).

11. Rawson, "Dealing with Disintegration," pp. 171–76.

12. Neil Henry, "Rebels, Rights Groups Attack Somalia," *Washington Post*, February 18, 1990, p. A23. On this period of urban terror see also Ali K. Galaydh, "Notes on the State of the Somali State," *Horn of Africa*, vol. 13 (January–June 1990), pp. 24–27.

13. Mohamed Sahnoun, *Somalia: The Missed Opportunities* (Washington: U.S. Institute of Peace Press, 1994), pp. 7–8.

14. The capacity of the international community to use external leverage in combination with internal protest to encourage political transition without state collapse was seen in Kenya (1993) and Malawi (1994).

15. *Horn of Africa Bulletin*, vol. 2 (June 1990), p. 26. Mohamed Osman Omar, *The Road to Zero: Somalia's Self-Destruction* (London: Haan, 1992), pp. 197–89; and Novati, "Italy in the Triangle of the Horn," p. 380, argues that Italy wanted to keep Siad Barre in the negotiations to avoid a "dangerous vacuum."

16. " 'Warring Factions' Encouraged to Attend Talks," Agence France-Presse, December 4, 1990, reprinted in Foreign Broadcast Information Service, *Daily Report: Sub-Saharan Africa*, December 6, 1990, pp. 7–8; *Horn of Africa Bulletin*, vol. 2 (December 1990), p. 27, and vol. 3 (January–February 1991), p. 2.

17. Samuel M. Makinda, *Seeking Peace from Chaos: Humanitarian Intervention in Somalia* (Boulder: Lynne Rienner, 1993), pp. 26–27.

18. For a first-hand account see Ambassador James K. Bishop, "Escape from Mogadishu," *Foreign Service Journal*, vol. 6 (March 1991), pp. 26–31. The evacuation was conducted by ships on their way to the Gulf in preparation for Desert Storm.

19. Cited in Daniel Volman, "Africa and the New World Order," *Journal of Modern African Studies*, vol. 31 (March 1993), p. 7.

20. Drysdale, *Whatever Happened to Somalia?*, p. 33; "Somalia: A Fight to the Death?" *News from Africa Watch*, New York, February 13, 1992, p. 5; and Samuel M. Makinda, *Seeking Peace from Chaos: Humanitarian Intervention in Somalia* (Boulder: Lynne Rienner, 1993), pp. 31–33.

21. See the statements by Mohamed Sahnoun in Thomas W. Lippman, "U.N. Chief Faulted in Somalia Mess," *Washington Post*, August 29, 1994, p. A16.

22. Ray Bonner, "Why We Went," *Mother Jones*, vol. 18 (March–April 1993), p. 55.

23. Ambassador Mario Sica, quoted in John G. Sommer, *Hope Restored? Humanitarian Aid in Somalia, 1990–1994* (Washington: Refugee Policy Group, November 1994), p. 9.

24. For a thorough discussion of the various estimated numbers of victims see Steven Hansch and others, *Excess Mortality and the Impact of Health Intervention in the Somalia Humanitarian Emergency* (Washington: Refugee Policy Group, 1994). See Francis M. Deng, *Protecting the Dispossessed: A Challenge for the International Community* (Brookings, 1993), pp. 51–63, for an account of internal displacement.

25. Statement by Andrew Natsios, assistant administrator for food and humanitarian assistance, U.S. Agency for International Development, before the House Select Committee on Hunger, January 30, 1992.

26. UN Security Council Resolution 733 (January 23, 1992). On issues relating to invoking Chapter VII and internal conflicts see Lori Fisler Damrosch, "Changing Conceptions of Intervention in International Law," in Laura W. Reed and Carl Kaysen, eds., *Emerging Norms of Justified Intervention* (Cambridge, Mass.: American Academy of Arts and Science, 1993), p. 105.

27. Clark, "Debacle in Somalia," p. 119; Trevor Rowe, "Aid to Somalia Stymied," *Washington Post*, July 29,1992, p. A1;and Jane Perlez, "Somalia Self-Destructs, and the World Looks On," *New York Times*, December 29, 1991, p. D4; Assistant Secretary of State Herman J. Cohen, testimony in "Emergency Situation in Zaire and Somalia," Hearings before the Africa Subcommittee of the Senate Foreign Relations Committee on Somalia and Zaire, 102 Cong. 2 sess. (Government Printing Office, 1992). The mixed signals coming from Washington reflected in part a split between officials such as Cohen and Natsios, who were pushing for engagement, and others such as Assistant Secretary for International Organization Affairs John Bolton and National Security Adviser Brent Scowcroft who were wary of increased involvement.

28. Rakiya Omaar, "Somalia: At War with Itself," *Current History*, vol. 91 (May 1992), pp. 233–39; and "Somalia: A Fight to the Death?" *News from Africa Watch*, New York, February 13, 1992, pp. 7–10.

29. Jeffrey Clark, "Debacle in Somalia," *Foreign Affairs*, vol. 72 (1993), p. 115.

30. Paul Lewis, "Security Council Weighs Role in Somali Civil War," *New York Times*, March 18, 1992, p. A9. The U.S. administration was reluctant to accept expanded peacekeeping responsibilities because of congressional objections to the cost.

31. "Security Council Establishes New UN Operation in Somalia," *UN Chronicle*, vol. 29 (September 1992), pp. 13–15.

32. "Somalia: Time to Take Stock," *Africa Confidential*, vol. 33 (April 17, 1992), pp. 4–5; and Rakiya Omaar and Alex de Waal, "Who Prolongs Somalia's Agony?" *New York Times*, February 26, 1992, p. A21.

33. Thomas J. Callahan, "Some Observations on Somalia's Past and Future," *CSIS Africa Notes*, no. 158 (March 1994), p. 2.

34. Jane Perlez, "Deaths in Somalia Outpace Delivery of Food," *New York Times*, July 19, 1992, p. A1. The International Committee for the Red Cross organized Perlez's trip and played a critical role in encouraging coverage.

35. "The Hell Called Somalia," editorial, *New York Times*, July 23, 1992, p. A14.

36. See, for example, Senate Resolution 115 that Congress passed on June 28, 1991. *Congressional Record*, June 28, 1991, p.S9214. Reed Kramer, "Somalia Rescue Begins," *Africa News*, vol. 36 (August 3–16, 1992), pp. 1–2.

37. Trevor Rowe, "Aid to Somalia Stymied," *Washington Post*, July 29, 1992, p. A1.

38. Paul Lewis, "U.S. Offering Plan for Somali Relief," *New York Times*, September 18, 1992, p. A10.

39. Ken Menkhaus and Louis Ortmayer, "Key Decisions in the Somalia Intervention."

40. Keith Richburg, "U.N. Envoy for Somalia Resigns Post, Blames Bureaucracy," *Washington Post*, October 30, 1992, p. A31; Jane Perlez, "Top U.N. Relief Official in Somalia Quits Over Dispute," *New York Times*, October 28, 1992, p. A6; and Ray Bonner, "Why We Went," *Mother Jones*, vol. 18 (March–April 1993), pp. 54–60.

41. "UN Operation in Somalia Strengthened," *UN Chronicle*, vol. 29 (December 1992), pp. 4–8.

42. Todd Shields, "U.N. Troops in Somalia: Frustration Every Day," *Washington Post*, December 3, 1992, p. A1.

43. David Brown, "Data Indicates Somali Famine among Worst," *Washington Post*, January 9, 1993, p. A17.

44. Jeffrey Clarke, "Debacle in Somalia: Failure of the Collective Response," in Lori Fisler Damrosch, ed., *Enforcing Restraint: Collective Intervention in Internal Conflicts* (New York: Council on Foreign Relations, 1993), p. 213. The United Nations estimated 500,000 deaths as a result of famine. For an evaluation of various estimates see Steven Hansch and others, *Excess Mortality and the Impact of Health Interventions in the Somalia Humanitarian Emergency* (Washington: Refugee Policy Group, 1994).

45. Don Oberdorfer, "The Path to Intervention: A Massive Tragedy 'We Could Do Something About,'" *Washington Post*, December 6, 1992, p. A1.

46. Michael R. Gordon, "Somali Aid Plan Is Called Most Ambitious Option," *New York Times*, November 28, 1992, p. A6.

47. Oberdorfer, "The Path to Intervention."

48. For details see Ken Menkhaus and Louis Ortmayer, "Key Decisions in the Somalia Intervention," typescript.

49. "Operation Restore Hope: UN-Mandated Force Seeks to Halt Tragedy," *UN Chronicle*, vol. 30 (March 1993), p. 16; and John R. Bolton, "Wrong Turn in Somalia," *Foreign Affairs*, vol. 73 (January–February 1994), pp. 59–60.

50. Trevor Rowe, "U.N. Management Urged for Somalia," *Washington Post*, November 28, 1992, p. A1.

51. UN Security Resolution 794 (December 3, 1992).

52. Ibid.

53. Cited in Bolton, "Wrong Turn in Somalia," p. 60.

54. Text of President Bush's statement, *Washington Post*, December 5, 1992, p. A16.

Chapter Four

1. Walter S. Clarke, "Testing the World's Resolve in Somalia," *Parameters*, vol. 23 (Winter 1993–94), p. 42.

2. Keith B. Richburg, "U.S. Envoy Tells Somali Warlords Not to Interfere," *Washington Post*, December 8, 1992, p. A1.

3. This is the conclusion of Robert Oakley and John Hirsch, *Somalia and Operation* Restore Hope*: Reflections on Peacemaking and Peacekeeping* (Washington: U.S. Institute of Peace Press, forthcoming).

4. John Drysdale, adviser to UNOSOM, "Some Reasons Why UNOSOM Continues to have Problems in its Relations with Major Somali Political Leaders and Suggestions as to How Credibility Could Be Restored," December 22, 1992.

5. William Claiborne and Keith B. Richburg, "U.S. Envoy Oakley Arranges Talks between Two Top Somali Warlords," *Washington Post,* December 11, 1992, p. A1; William Claiborne and Barton Gellman, "Rival Warlords Sign Peace Pact in Somalia," *Washington Post*, December 12,1992, p. A1; and "Details of Agreement between Aidid, Ali Mahdi," Mogadishu Voice of the Somali Republic in Somali, December 11, 1992, translated and reprinted in Foreign Broadcast Information Service, *Daily Report: Sub-Saharan Africa*, December 14, 1992, p. 13.

6. William Claiborne and Barton Gellman, "Rival Warlords Sign Peace Pact in Somalia," *Washington Post*, December 12, 1992, p. A1.

7. Keith B. Richburg, "2 Somali Warlords Say Peace Is at Hand," *Washington Post*, December 28, 1992, p. A9.

8. UN document S/25126, Letter dated January 19,1993, from the Permanent Representative of the United States of America to the United Nations Addressed to the President of the Security Council. See also Stuart Auerbach, "Oakley Calls Mission in Somalia a Success," *Washington Post*, March 3, 1993, p. A19.

9. Barton Gellman and William Claiborne, "Marines Enter Key Somali City," *Washington Post*, December 16, 1992, p. A1.

10. Don Oberdorfer, "U.S. Ahead of Schedule in Somalia," *Washington Post*, December 30, 1992, p. A1.

11. Don Oberdorfer, "Envoy to Somalia Follows Own Script," *Washington Post*, December 11, 1992, p. A47.

12. Jane Perlez, "Witnesses Report a Somali Massacre before U.S. Arrival," *New York Times*, December 29, 1992, p. A1.

13. Jane Perlez, "Witnesses Report a Somali Massacre before U.S. Arrival," *New York Times*, December 29, 1992, p. A1; Médecins sans Frontières president Reginald Moreels referred to these killings as "clannic cleaning." See also the account by British UNICEF fieldworker Sean Devereux in Barton Gellman, "Killings Spur Quicker Pace for Marines," *Washington Post*, December 21, 1992, p. A16. Devereux later was murdered in Kismayu, shot twice in the back of the head on January 2, 1993. The U.S. military believed it knew who was responsible, but no actions were taken. See Keith Richburg, "Getting Away with Murder in Somalia," *Washington Post*, April 8, 1993, p. A31.

14. John Lancaster, "General Bars Disarming Somali Clans," *Washington Post*, December 15, 1992, p. A1.

15. For a critique of U.S. reluctance to disarm see Rakiya Omaar and Alex de Waal, *Somalia: Operation Restore Hope: A Preliminary Assessment* (London: African Rights, May 1993), pp. 20–27. See also Robert M. Press, "U.S. Marines in Somalia Face Dilemma Over Disarmament," *Christian Science Monitor*, December 14, 1992, p. 1; and Michael R. Gordon, "Marines Will Find Somalia Awash in Weapons, Some of Them Supplied by the U.S.," *New York Times*, December 9, 1992, p. A17.

16. William Claiborne and Barton Gellman, "Rival Warlords Sign Peace Pact in Somalia," *Washington Post*, December 12, 1992, p. A1.

17. Keith B. Richburg, "2 Somali Warlords Say Peace is at Hand," *Washington Post*, December 28, 1992, p. A9.

18. John Lancaster and Keith B. Richburg, "Marines Seize Tons of Weapons in Raid on Mogadishu Bazaar," *Washington Post*, January 12, 1993, p. A12; and Kenneth Noble, "Troops in Somalia Raid Big Arsenal," *New York Times*, January 12, 1993, p. A3. For an account of the frustrations felt by marines engaged in such searches see Diana Jean Schemo, "Amid 'Hatfields and McCoys,' Marines Disarm the Somalis," *New York Times*, February 16, 1993, p. A1.

19. Rakiya Omaar and Alex de Waal, *Operation Restore Hope: A Preliminary Assessment* (London: African Rights, May 1993), pp. 24–25.

20. Keith B. Richburg, "U.S. to Set Up Somali Police Unit," *Washington Post*, January 29, 1993, p. A17.

21. Kenneth B. Noble, "Somalia Clans Hold Talks on a Joint Police Force," *New York Times*, January 14, 1993, p. A5.

22. Keith B. Richburg, "2 Somali Warlords Say Peace Is at Hand," *Washington Post*, December 28, 1992, p. A9.

23. Ken Menkhaus, "Getting Out vs. Getting Through: U.S. and U.N. Policies in Somalia," *Middle East Policy*, vol. 3 (1994), p. 149.

24. Don Oberdorfer, "U.S. Ahead of Schedule in Somalia," *Washington Post*, December 30, 1992, p. A1. Two senior diplomats from the United States did attend: Deputy Assistant Secretary of State for African Affairs Robert Houdek and Ambassador Irvin Hicks from the U.S. Mission to the United Nations in New York.

25. Keith B. Richburg, "U.S. Envoy in Somalia Viewed as Linchpin of Reconciliation," *Washington Post*, February 2, 1993, p. A14; and Stuart Auerbach, "Oakley Laments Exit before U.S. Troops," *Washington Post*, March 3, 1993, p. A19.

26. Keith Richburg, "American Casualties in Somalia: A Policy Time Bomb Explodes," *Washington Post*, August 12, 1993, p. A1.

27. *The Situation in Somalia: Progress Report of the Secretary General*, S/25168 (United Nations, January 26, 1993).

28. Paul Lewis, "Somali Clan Chiefs Are to Meet Today," *New York Times*, January 4, 1993, p. A6.

29. Stanley Meisler, "Somali Leader Rips U.N., Stalls Talks," *Los Angeles Times*, January 6, 1993, p. A6.

30. In addition to the United Nations, the Secretaries General of the League of

Arab States, the Organization of African Unity, and the Organization of the Islamic Conference participated in the Addis Ababa talks.

31. In fact, the agreements were signed by fifteen Somalis. The Somali Democratic Movement had split, and both Abdi Muse Mayo and Col. Maohmed Nur Aliyou signed as chairmen.

32. Paul Lewis, "Somali Factions Take a Tentative Step Toward Reconciliation," *New York Times*, January 8, 1993, p. A8; Reuters, "Somalia Factions Sign a Truce Pact," *New York Times*, January 16, 1993, p. A2; and Jennifer Parmelee, "Somali Warlord Slows Progress toward Peace," *Washington Post*, January 12, 1993, p. 14.

33. Kenneth B. Noble, "400 U.S. Marines Attack Compound of Somali Gunmen," *New York Times*, January 8, 1993, p. A1.

34. *The Situation in Somalia: Progress Report of the Secretary General*, S/25168 (United Nations, January 26, 1993), annex II, III, and IV. See also John Drysdale, *Whatever Happened to Somalia?* (London: Haan, 1994), pp. 107–09.

35. SNU, "The Addis Ababa Agreement: Agreeing to Disagree," *Somalia News Update*, vol. 2 (January 19, 1993); and "Somalia: Who's Who," *Economist*, January 23, 1993, pp. 41–42.

36. "Next Steps in Somalia," *Financial Times*, January 4, 1993, p. 21; and Stanley Meisler, "Peace Talks Continue," *Los Angeles Times*, January 7, 1993, p. A3.

37. Walter S. Clarke, "Testing the World's Resolve," *Parameters*, vol. 23 (Winter 1993–94), p. 50.

38. SNU, "SNU Comment: UN as an Obstacle to Peace in Somalia," *Somalia News Update*, vol. 2 (February 4, 1993).

39. Africa Watch, "Somalia Beyond the Warlords: The Need for a Verdict on Human Rights Abuses," *News from Africa Watch*, vol. 5 (March 7, 1993), p. 2.

40. "30,000-Strong UN Force Steps in to 'Restore Hope,'" *UN Chronicle*, vol. 30 (June 1993), p. 17.

41. *Further Report of the Secretary-General Submitted in Pursuance of Paragraphs 18 and 19 of Resolution 794,* S/25354 (United Nations, March 3,1993), p. 4. See also Samuel M. Makinda, *Seeking Peace from Chaos: Humanitarian Intervention in Somalia* (Boulder: Lynne Rienner for the International Peace Academy, 1993), pp. 35, 65.

42. Rakiya Omaar, "Somalia: The Best Chance for Peace," *Africa Report*, vol. 38 (May–June 1993), pp. 45–48; and Rakiya Omaar, "Somaliland: One Thorn Bush at a Time," *Current History*, vol. 93 (May 1994), pp. 232–36; and Ahmed Samatar, "The Curse of Allah: Civic Disembowelment and the Collapse of the State in Somalia," in Ahmed Samatar, ed., *The Somali Challenge: From Catastrophe to Renewal?* (Boulder: Lynne Rienner, 1994), pp. 122–25.

43. "New President, Vice President Elected in Somaliland," AFP, Agence France-Presse, May 8, 1993, reprinted in Foreign Broadcast Information Service, *Daily Report: Sub-Saharan Africa*, May 10, 1993, p. 6.

44. Rakiya Omaar, "Somaliland: One Thorn Bush at a Time," *Current History*, vol. 93 (May 1994), pp. 232–36; memorandum from Kouyate to Howe, "The Boroma Conference," April 9, 1993; memorandum from Kouyate to Howe, "Meeting with DCM Walter Clarke of USLO/Implementation of Addis Agreement/Boroma Conference in Somaliland," April 7, 1993.

45. Quoted in Jennifer Parmelee, "Somali Warlord Slows Progress toward Peace," *Washington Post*, January 12, 1993, p. A14.

46. Ibid.

47. Quoted ibid.

48. Ibrahim Bursalid, founder of Soma Action, quoted in Alexandra Tuttle, "Somalia and the Spoils of Power," *Wall Street Journal*, January 5, 1993, p. A14.

49. Howard Witt, "Despite Claims by U.S., Somalia Is Still a Mess," *Chicago Tribune*, February 28, 1993, sec. 4, p. 1.

50. Cited in Diana Jean Schemo, "Nearly Everything in Somalia Is Now Up for Grabs," *New York Times*, February 21, 1993, p. A3.

51. Oakley stated that the Cobras "took care of Morgan for not respecting the cease-fire, continuing to move south after we told him to stop, and for general misbehavior." Quoted in Diana Jean Schemo, "U.S. Copters Attack Rebel Force in Southern Somalia," *New York Times*, January 26, 1993, p. A3.

52. AP, "U.S. Tells Clan's Forces to Leave Somali Port," *New York Times*, February 24, 1993, p. A7. Of all the militia leaders, Oakley reserved special animus for Morgan. He referred to Morgan as "the only individual I know personally who is a mass murderer." Quoted in Diana Jean Schemo, "Bur Koy Journal: Somali Warlords Recruited (It's the Price of Peace)," *New York Times*, January 28, 1993, p. A4; and Molly Moore, "Deep in the Desert with a Somali Militia," *Washington Post*, February 23, 1993.

53. *Further Report of the Secretary-General Submitted in Pursuance of Paragraphs 18 and 19 of Resolution 794*, S/25354 (United Nations, March 3, 1994), para 6.

54. Keith B. Richburg, "Somali Warlords' Successors Gingerly Emerge," *Washington Post*, January 30, 1993, p. A15.

55. Diana Jean Schemo, "Nearly Everything in Somalia Is Now Up for Grabs," *New York Times*, February 21, 1993, p. A3. See also Daniel Williams and John Lancaster, "Somali Violence May Delay U.S. Withdrawal," *Washington Post*, February 26, 1993, p. A1; and "Somalia: The UN Trundles into Action," *Africa Confidential*, March 19, 1993, p. 1.

56. Drysdale, *Whatever Happened to Somalia?*, pp. 13, 110.

57. "Upsurge in Fighting," *Indian Ocean Newsletter*, February 27, 1993, p. 2; and "Somalia: The UN Trundles into Action," *Africa Confidential*, vol. 34 (March 19, 1993), p. 2.

58. Walter S. Clarke, "Testing the World's Resolve in Somalia," *Parameters*, vol. 23 (Winter 1993–94), p. 49; and "Somalia: NGO's Take a Gentle Bow," *Indian Ocean Newsletter* (April 17, 1993), pp. 1–2.

59. "30,000-Strong UN Force Steps in to 'Restore Hope,'" *UN Chronicle*, vol. 30 (June 1993), pp. 16–17; and *Further Report of the Secretary-General*. The UN report noted that the ad hoc committee's deliberations in Mogadishu were interrupted for three days in February "owing to rioting and fighting."

60. *Further Report of the Secretary-General*, para. 16.

61. SNU, "Eliasson's Speech to the Conference," *Somalia News Update*, vol. 2 (March 11, 1993).

62. SNU, "Addis 'Reconciliation' Conference Opened," *Somalia News Update*, vol. 2 (March 16, 1993).

63. Walter S. Clarke, "Testing the World's Resolve in Somalia," *Parameters*, vol. 23 (Winter 1993–94), p. 51.

64. The agreement was "unanimously endorsed" by the full conference, including nonmilitia representatives, after it had been finalized in closed door talks with militia leaders. "Secretary-General Welcomes Signing of Agreement on National Reconciliation by Somali Participants at Conference in Addis Ababa," press release, SG/SM/4953/SOM/18 (United Nations, March 29, 1993).

65. Jennifer Parmelee, "Waltzing with Warlords," *Washington Post*, June 20, 1993, p. C1.

66. Ibid.

67. "Talks against Bellicose Background," *Indian Ocean Newsletter*, March 20, 1993, p. 3; and SNU, "Addis 'Reconciliation' Conference Opened," *Somalia News Update*, vol.2 (March 16, 1993).

68. "Wresting an Agreement," *Indian Ocean Newsletter*, March 27, 1993, p. 2.

69. Donatella Lorch, "Talks On Somalia Suspended by U.N.," *New York Times*, March 18, 1993, p. A7; and Voice of Ethiopia in Foreign Broadcast Information Service, *Daily Report: Sub-Saharan Africa*; "Kismaayo Committee Returns," March 22, 1993, p. 1; and *The Situation in Somalia: Progress Report of the Secretary General*, S/25168 (United Nations, January 26, 1993), p. 2.

70. AP, "U.S. Tells Clan's Forces to Leave Somali Port," *New York Times*, February 24, 1993, p. A7.

71. African Rights, *Somalia: Human Rights Abuses by the United Nations Forces* (London: African Rights, July 1993), pp. 17, 25.

72. John Burgess, "Somali Team Investigates Battle at Port," *Washington Post*, March 20, 1993, p. A19; John Burgess, "U.S. Troops Patrol Somali Port City in Show of Force to Feuding Factions," *Washington Post*, March 19, 1993, p. A48; Jennifer Parmelee, "Somali Peace Talks Suspended as Result of Fighting in Southern Town," *Washington Post*, March 18, 1993, p. A32; and Donatella Lorch, "Talks on Somalia Suspended by U.N.," *New York Times*, March 18, 1993, p. A7.

73. Deputy Special Representative Lansana Kouyate to Special Representative Jonathan Howe, "The First Session of the Conference on National Reconciliation in Somalia," April 4, 1993. This internal UNOSOM memo relates Kouyate's perspective on the value of the Addis Ababa agreement.

74. The Addis Ababa agreement is reprinted in *The UN and the Situation in Somalia: Reference Paper* (New York: UN Department of Public Information, March 1994), p. 11. See also "Factions Agree on Interim Government, Treaty," BBC, March 28, 1993, reprinted in Foreign Broadcast Information Service, *Daily Report:Sub-Saharan Africa*, March 29, 1993, p. 1; and Donatella Lorch, "Somalia's Leaders Reach Agreement," *New York Times,* March 29, 1993, p. A5.

75. Memorandum from Kouyate to Howe, "The First Session of the Conference on National Reconciliation in Somalia."

76. The Addis Ababa agreement is reprinted in *The UN and the Situation in Somalia: Reference Paper* (New York: UN Department of Information, March 1994),

p. 11. For analysis see Ken Menkhaus, "Getting Out vs. Getting Through: U.S. and U.N. Policies in Somalia," *Middle East Policy*, vol. 3 (1994), p. 150.

77. Jonathan Stevenson, "Hope Restored in Somalia?" *Foreign Policy*, no. 91 (Summer 1993), pp. 141–42, 150.

78. Cited in Donatella Lorch, "Somalia's Leaders Reach Agreement," *New York Times*, March 29, 1993, p. A5.

79. SNU, "The Addis Ababa Agreement: The Ultimate Bribe," *Somalia News Update*, vol. 2 (March 30, 1993).

80. This section is cowritten with John Wesley Days.

81. Keith B. Richburg, "Changeover in Somalia Taking Shape," *Washington Post*, March 10, 1993, p. A21.

82. Refugee Policy Group, *Humanitarian Aid in Somalia* (September 1994), pp. 37–38.

83. UN Security Council Resolution 814 (March 26, 1993); "Security Council Authorizes Enforcement Action by UNOSOM II to Secure Humanitarian Relief Operations throughout Somalia," press release, SC/5573, United Nations, March 26, 1993; "30,000-Strong UN Force Steps in to 'Restore Hope,'" *UN Chronicle*, vol. 30 (June 1993), pp. 13–17.

84. "Secretary-General Welcomes Signing of Agreement on National Reconciliation by Somali Participants at Conference in Addis Ababa," press release, SG/SM/4953, SOM/18, United Nations, March 29, 1993.

85. The Addis Ababa agreement is reprinted in *The UN and the Situation in Somalia*, p. 11.

86. Memorandum from Kouyate to Howe, "The First Session of the Conference on National Reconciliation in Somalia," April 4, 1993; and memorandum from Kouyate to Howe, "Views and Assessment on How UNOSOM Will Assist in the Implementation of the Agreement," April 5, 1993.

87. The request for a new identity came from Jess. See Keith B. Richburg, "Somali Warlords Shift Roles," *Washington Post*, May 11, 1993, p. A12.

88. Memorandum from Lansana Kouyate to Jonathan Howe, "UNOSOM Role in the Implementation of the Addis Ababa Agreement," April 23, 1993; and memorandum from Kouyate to Howe, "Follow-up on the Implementation of the Addis Ababa Agreement," April 15, 1993.

89. Kouyate to Howe, "Meeting with DCM Walter Clarke of USLO/Implementation of Addis Agreement/Boroma Conference in Somaliland," April 7, 1993. See Ken Menkhaus, "Getting Out Vs. Getting Through: U.S. and U.N. Policies in Somalia," *Middle East Policy*, vol. 3 (1994), p. 150.

90. Kouyate to Howe, untitled memo, April 1, 1993; Kouyate to Howe, "Meeting with American Ambassador Gosende," April 3, 1993. In a memo to the files Kouyate suggested that "as a matter of principle, to have a bad solution is better than no solution in situations like Somalia." "Notes for the File: Preliminary Discussions between the CHA and the DSRSG," April 5, 1993.

91. Kouyate to Howe, "Meetings with Ali Mahdi/Addis Agreement/Kismayo," April 4, 1993.

92. Drysdale, *Whatever Happened to Somalia?*, p. 7.

93. Memo from Lansana Kouyate, DSRSG to Admiral Howe, SRSG, "Meeting on April 28 with Ambassador Bob Gosende," nd.

94. The United States commissioned a report on the steps necessary to reestablish the Somali legal system. Martin R. Ganzglass, "Evaluation of the Judicial, Legal, and Penal Systems of Somalia: April 8–22, 1993."

95. Kouyate to Howe, "Trip to Bossaso/Discussions with the SSDF," undated report of May 10, 1993, trip. See also Geraldine Brooks, "The Test of Will: The U.N. Is Making Progress in Somalia, but Time Grows Short," *Wall Street Journal*, October 15, 1993, p. 1.

96. On the district council in Baidoa see Alison Mitchell, "Marines in Somalia Try to Rebuild a Town Council," *New York Times*, January 18, 1993, p. A3; and Keith B. Richburg, "Somalia's First Step," *Washington Post*, September 25, 1993, p. A1.

97. Keith B. Richburg, "Somalia's First Step," *Washington Post*, September 25, 1993, p. A1.

98. Donatella Lorch, "Far from Capital's Brutality, Another Somalia Finds Hope," *New York Times*, October 24, 1993, p. A1, details attempts by the Somali National Alliance to undermine the council in Baidoa. Generally see Ken Menkhaus, "Getting Out vs. Getting Through: U.S. and U.N. Policies in Somalia," *Middle East Policy*, vol. 3 (1994).

99. "Somalia: General Aideed Defies United Nations," *Indian Ocean Newsletter*, June 5, 1993, p. 4; and Walter S. Clarke, "Testing the World's Resolve in Somalia," *Parameters*, vol. 23 (Winter 1993–94), pp. 52–53. Aideed's supporters reportedly stole the tables and chairs from the UN site to prevent the meeting.

100. Drysdale, *Whatever Happened to Somalia?*, pp. 167–71.

101. Walter S. Clarke, "Testing the World's Resolve in Somalia," *Parameters*, vol. 13 (Winter 1993–94), p. 53.

102. Keith B. Richburg, "Mogadishu Erupts in Violence," *Washington Post*, June 6, 1993, p. A29.

103. Ken Menkhaus and Louis Ortmayer, "Key Decisions in the Somalia Intervention."

104. U.S. officials interpreted such threats as evidence that the militia leaders were feeling the pressure as the United States and the United Nations continued to marginalize them. Aideed used his radio to make harsh statements against the United States and the United Nations, accusing them of having "killed, maimed, raped, detained, tortured or harassed" Somalis and criticizing UN plans "to ignore or better yet marginalize, the warring factions and their leaders." Keith B. Richburg, "Americans in Somalia Face Threat," *Washington Post*, May 14, 1993, p. A36.

105. UN Security Council Resolution 837 (June 6, 1993); and "UNOSOM II Takes 'Decisive Action' to Restore Peace," *UN Chronicle*, vol. 30 (September 1993), pp. 4–7.

106. Barton Gellman, "U.S. Rhetoric Changed, but Hunt Persisted," *Washington Post*, October 7, 1993, p. A37.

107. Barton Gellman, "U.S. Rhetoric Changed, but Hunt Persisted"; Madeleine K. Albright, "Yes, There Is a Reason to Be in Somalia," op-ed, *New York Times*, August 10, 1993, p. A19; and "UNOSOM II Takes 'Decisive Action' to Restore

Peace," *UN Chronicle*, vol. 30 (September 1993), p. 5.

108. SNU, "Peace Accord on Kismayu and Jubaland," *Somalia News Update*, vol. 2 (August 8, 1993). The United Nations details its efforts outside Mogadishu in *Further Report of the Secretary-General Submitted in Pursuance of Paragraph 18 of Resolution 814*, S/26317 (United Nations, August 17, 1993). See also Donatella Lorch, "Far from Capital's Brutality, Another Somalia Finds Hope," *New York Times*, October 24, 1993, p. A1.

109. Robert M. Press, "Continued Assault on Somali Warlord May Backfire on UN," *Christian Science Monitor*, June 18, 1993, p. 7; and Keith B. Richburg, "U.N. Helicopter Assault in Somalia Targeted Aideed's Top Commanders," *Washington Post*, July 16, 1993, p. A1. The July 12 attack resulted in rioting that killed four journalists and a major rift between Italy and the United States over UN strategy.

110. Keith B. Richburg, "Criticism Mounts over Somali Raid," *Washington Post*, July 15, 1993, p. A21.

111. John Lancaster and Daniel Williams, "Elite U.S. Troops Going to Somalia," *Washington Post*, August 24, 1993, p. A1.

112. Speech by Secretary of Defense Les Aspin to the Center for Strategic and International Studies, Washington, August 27, 1993.

113. Sidney Blumenthal, "Why Are We in Somalia?" *New Yorker*, October 25, 1993, pp. 48–60; Elaine Sciolino, "Pentagon Alters Goals in Somalia, Signaling Failure," *New York Times*, September 28, 1993, p. A1; and Thomas E. Ricks and Robert S. Greenberger, "Clinton Seeks Graceful Exit from Somalia," *Wall Street Journal*, September 29, 1993, p. 3. President Clinton began to focus on Somalia in September following meetings with former president Jimmy Carter and Italian Prime Minister Carlo Ciampi. Following the Ciampi meeting Clinton stated his intention to develop a political initiative but when asked what the process would be responded, "Our position is not well enough formed yet to be characterized fairly." See Thomas W. Lippman and Barton Gellman, "A Humanitarian Gesture Turns Deadly," *Washington Post*, October 10, 1993, p. A1.

114. Keith B. Richburg, "U.S. Somalia Envoy Urged Policy Shift before 18 GIs Died," *Washington Post*, November 11, 1993, p. A39.

115. Rick Atkinson, "The Raid That Went Wrong: How An Elite U.S. Force Failed in Somalia," *Washington Post*, January 30, 1994, p. A1; Rick Atkinson, "Night of a Thousand Casualties: Battle Triggered U.S. Decision to Withdraw from Somalia," *Washington Post*, January 31, 1994, p. A1. For an account by the Department of Defense see the statements in U.S. Senate Committee in Current Military Operations, Hearings before the U.S. Senate Committee on Armed Services, August 6, October 4, 7, 12, 13, 1993, 103 Cong. 2 sess. (Government Printing Office, 1994).

116. Thomas L. Friedman, "The World: Harm's Way: U.S. Pays Dearly for an Education in Somalia," *New York Times*, October 10, 1993, p. E1.

117. Ann Devoy, "New Deployment Raises Confusion on U.S. Goals," *Washington Post*, October 6, 1994, p. A1. Sidney Blumenthal, "Why Are We In Somalia?" *New Yorker*, October 25, 1993, p. 51, characterized this briefing as "a spectacle

worthy of Abbott and Costello. . . . utterly bereft of direction." Thomas J. Callahan, "Some Observations On Somalia's Past and Future," *CSIS Africa Notes*, no. 158 (Washington: Center for Strategic and International Studies, March 1994), p. 7, wrote, "The briefing was a turning point in the U.S. involvement in Somalia. . . . Many members could have been assuaged . . . if the administration had appeared steadfast, explained its contingency plans in the face of increased Somali opposition, and indicated a clear course of action. Instead, members left the briefing with the sense of a policy adrift."

118. Sidney Blumenthal, "Why Are We in Somalia?" *New Yorker*, October 25, 1993, pp. 49–60, provides an insightful account of the reaction in Washington to the October 6 battle. Carroll J. Doherty, "Clinton Calms Rebellion on Hill by Retooling Somalia Mission," *Congressional Quarterly*, October 9, 1993, pp. 2750–51.

119. See transcript in *New York Times*, October 8, 1993, p. A15.

120. *Africa Research Bulletin*, vol. 30 (December 1993), p. 11275.

121. Julie Flint, "UN Soldiers Doomed to Stand and Stare as Warlords Run Mogadishu," *Guardian*, July 1994.

122. Keith B. Richburg, "Somalia Slips Back to Bloodshed," *Washington Post*, September 4, 1994, p. A1.

123. Robert M. Press, "US Somalia Pullout Seen Leading the Way to UN Withdrawal," *Christian Science Monitor*, August 30, 1994, p. 1; and I. M. Lewis, "White-Washing the UN's Failures in Somalia," *Somalia News Update*, vol. 3 (August 27, 1994), pp. 3–4.

124. Menkhaus, "Getting Out vs. Getting Through."

125. Conference Report, *The United Nations, Peacekeeping, and U.S. Policy in the Post–Cold War World* (Queenstown, Md.: Aspin Institute, 1994), p. 9.

126. Walter S. Clarke, "Testing the World's Resolve in Somalia," *Parameters*, vol. 23 (Winter 1993–94), p. 49.

Chapter Five

1. See A. I. Samatar, "The Exigencies of Self-Determination, Territorial Integrity, and Collective Self-Reliance," in Nzongola-Ntalaja, ed., *Conflict and Peace in the Horn of Africa* (Atlanta, Ga.: African Studies Association, 1991).

2. Faisal Omer's composition is titled, *Laagey* (Money) and came to Ahmed Samatar's attention in 1985.

3. Aiden Southall, "'The Rain Fell on Its Own'—The Alur Theory of Development and Its Western Counterparts," *African Studies Review*, vol. 31 (September 1988), p. 6.

4. For more on this, see Ahmed I. Samatar, "The Curse of Allah: Civic Disembowelment and the Collapse of the State in Somalia," in Ahmed I. Samatar, ed., *The Somali Challenge: From Catastrophe to Renewal?* (Boulder: Lynne Rienner, 1994), p. 138.

Appendix A

1. The role played by the United States in assisting the transition that brought the Eritrean Peoples Liberation Front and the Ethiopian Peoples Revolutionary Democratic Front to power in 1991 is an example. See Terrence Lyons, "Great Powers and Conflict Reduction in the Horn of Africa," in I. William Zartman, ed., *Cooperative Security: Reducing Third World Wars* (Syracuse University Press, forthcoming). Others called for international support for the Rwandan Patriotic Front's efforts to consolidate its control following the genocide in Rwanda. See the statement by Roger Winter, "Rapid U.S. Support for New Rwandan Government Could Alleviate Humanitarian Emergency," *News From the U.S. Committee for Refugees*, July 20, 1994.

2. On the trade-offs between accountability and reconciliation generally see Stephen John Stedman, "Peace in Civil War: A Dilemma," *Brookings Review*, vol. 12 (Fall 1994), p. 46.

3. The characterization was made of Aideed. Said S. Samatar, "How to Save Somalia," op-ed, *Washington Post*, December 1, 1992, p. A19.

4. Aleksa Djilas, "A Profile of Slobodan Milosevic," *Foreign Affairs*, vol. 72 (Summer 1993), p. 88. See also John G. Ruggie, "The United Nations: Stuck in a Fog between Peacekeeping and Enforcement," in William H. Lewis, ed., *Peacekeeping: The Way Ahead?*, McNair Paper 25 (Washington: Institute for National Security Studies, November 1993).

5. Ken Menkhaus and Terrence Lyons, "What Are the Lessons to Be Learned from Somalia?" *CSIS Africa Notes*, no. 144 (Washington: Center for Strategic and International Studies, January 1993), p. 8. I have benefited from discussions with Menkhaus on this point.

6. Terrence Lyons, "Next Steps in Somalia," *Brookings Review*, vol.12 (Spring 1993), p. 46.

7. Ruggie, "The United Nations: Stuck in a Fog," p. 7.

8. Brian Hall, "Blue Helmets, Empty Guns," *New York Times Sunday Magazine*, January 2, 1994, p. 24.

Appendix B

1. For more information on these groups see Ken Menkhaus and Terrence Lyons, "What Are the Lessons to Be Learned from Somalia?" *CSIS Africa Notes*, no. 144 (Washington: Center for Strategic and International Studies, January 1993), p. 6; and "Forces and Factions," *Africa Confidential*, December 18, 1992, p. 3.